THE UNIVERSITY IN AFRICA AND DEMOCRATIC CITIZENSHIP
Hothouse or Training Ground?

Report on Student Surveys conducted at the University of Nairobi, Kenya, the University of Cape Town, South Africa, and the University of Dar es Salaam, Tanzania

Thierry M Luescher-Mamashela
with Sam Kiiru, Robert Mattes, Angolwisye Mwollo-ntallima, Njuguna Ng'ethe and Michelle Romo

Published by the Centre for Higher Education Transformation (CHET),
House Vincent, First Floor, 10 Brodie Road, Wynberg Mews, Wynberg, 7800
Telephone: +27(0)21 763-7100 | Fax: +27(0)21 763-7117
E-mail: chet@chet.org.za | www.chet.org.za

© CHET 2011

ISBN 978-1-920355-67-8

Produced by COMPRESS.dsl | www.compressdsl.com

Cover illustration by Raymond Oberholzer

Distributed by African Minds
4 Eccleston Place, Somerset West, 7130, South Africa
info@africanminds.co.za
www.africanminds.co.za

For orders from outside Africa:
African Books Collective
PO Box 721, Oxford OX1 9EN, UK
orders@africanbookscollective.com
www.africanbookscollective.com

Contents

Acknowledgements v

The Project Group vii

Executive Summary ix

CHAPTER 1: HERANA Higher Education and Democracy:
The Student Governance Surveys 1
1.1 Project overview 1
1.2 Analytical framework of the study 3
1.3 Research questions 12
1.4 Survey design and methods 14
1.5 Overview of the report 19

CHAPTER 2: Background and Context:
Three Countries, Universities and Student Bodies 21
2.1 Governance in Kenya, South Africa, and Tanzania in international comparison 21
2.2 Democracy in Kenya, the University of Nairobi and student politics 22
2.3 Democracy in South Africa, the University of Cape Town and student politics 26
2.4 Democracy in Tanzania, the University of Dar es Salaam and student politics 30
2.5 Profile of the three student bodies 33

CHAPTER 3: Students' Demand for Democracy and Freedom 43
3.1 Introduction 43
3.2 Awareness of 'democracy' 43
3.3 Preference for democracy over other regime types 49
3.4 Demand for political freedoms 54
3.5 Students as committed democrats? 56
3.6 Summary and conclusion 60

CHAPTER 4: Students' Perception of the Supply of Democracy
and Democratic Consolidation — 63
4.1 Introduction — 63
4.2 Perception of the current regime — 64
4.3 Has multi-party democracy supplied more political freedoms? — 69
4.4 Students as transformative democrats? — 72
4.5 Summary and conclusion — 81

CHAPTER 5: Students' Political Engagement and Behaviour — 83
5.1 Students' cognitive engagement with politics — 83
5.2 Students' political participation — 91
5.3 Students as active citizens? — 97
5.4 Summary and conclusion — 102

CHAPTER 6: Student Politics and the University:
Implications and Recommendations — 105
6.1 Overview of the findings — 105
6.2 Enhancing the university's training ground potential — 106

References — 112
Appendices — 117

Acknowledgements

In the past two decades, many African nations embarked on transitions to democracy, putting into place key political institutions that allow for competitive multi-party elections and liberalising the public realm. In order for democracy to consolidate, however, not only appropriate political institutions are needed; democracy requires democrats to be sustainable. To what extent and how higher education in Africa makes a contribution to democratic citizenship development has remained an open question.

It took a consultation and discussion period of almost three years between the Centre for Higher Education Transformation (CHET), senior researchers and the US Partnership for Higher Education in Africa to establish the Higher Education Research and Advocacy Network in Africa (HERANA).[1] Credit must be given to the US Partnership for supporting such a complex and potentially controversial project – and one which would not easily have been funded by a single foundation. Having on board the Ford Foundation, the Carnegie Corporation of New York, the Rockefeller Foundation and the Kresge Foundation contributed to the credibility of the project amongst higher education leaders and academics. A special word of thanks must go to Dr John Butler-Adam (Ford), who 'steered' the Partnership in this project, and to Dr Claudia Frittelli (Carnegie), who participated actively throughout.

The capacity-building component of HERANA is the Higher Education Masters in Africa, run jointly between the universities of the Western Cape, Makerere and Oslo, with students from eight African countries. The Masters programme is funded by the NOMA programme of the Norwegian Agency for Development Cooperation (NORAD) with Ms Tove Kivil a constant source of support.

We must acknowledge the fortuitous coincidence of HERANA and *University World News* starting at almost the same time. *University World News*, with its 30 000 readers, around 14 000 of whom subscribe to the Africa edition, has been a source of information for our project and a distribution resource.

For the purpose of this study, Afrobarometer methodology has been adapted and certain Afrobarometer data used in comparative analyses. We are grateful to the Afrobarometer for availing these to us.

We also acknowledge the comments received by various critical reviewers on parts or the full draft of this report.

---

[1] For a description of the various HERANA project components, participants and publications, visit the website at http://www.chet.org.za/programmes/herana/.

Finally, our thanks go to the Board of CHET, which not only expressed confidence in the CHET leadership, but participated in consultations to establish HERANA. Two CHET Board members who participated actively in the project are Prof. Teboho Moja (Chair of the Board, New York University) and Dr Esi Sutherland-Addy (University of Ghana).

The Project Group

Academic advisers	Prof. Robert Mattes (University of Cape Town)
	Prof. Njuguna Ng'ethe (University of Nairobi)
Senior researcher	Dr Thierry Luescher-Mamashela (University of the Western Cape)
Researcher	Mr Sam Kiiru (University of Nairobi)
Research trainees	Mr Angolwisye Mwollo-ntallima (University of the Western Cape)
	Mr Danga Mughogho (University of Cape Town)
	Ms Michelle Romo (University of Cape Town)
Project assistance	Ms Angela Mias (CHET Administrator)
	Ms Tracy Bailey (CHET)
	Ms Kathy Graham and Ms Marlene Titus (Funds Management)
External commentators	Dr Cherrel Africa (University of the Western Cape)
	Prof. Daniel Mkude (University of Dar es Salaam)
	Prof. Mokubung Nkomo (University of Pretoria)
University contacts	**Cape Town**: Prof. Danie Visser (DVC Research), Ms Moonira Khan (Executive Director: Student Affairs), Ms Edwina Goliath (Director: Student Development Office), Mr Jerome September (Manager: Student Governance & Leadership), Mr Thami Ledwaba (SRC Academic Officer)
	Dar es Salaam: Prof. Yunus D. Mgaya (DVC Administration), Dr Martha Qorro (Dean of Students), Dr Theodora Bali (Director: Student Governance Office of the Dean of Students), Prof. Daniel Mkude (Department of Linguistics), Dr Kitila Mkumbo (former DARUSO President, now Department of Educational Psychology and Curriculum Studies), Mr Anthony Machibya (DARUSO President 2008/2009)
	Nairobi: Prof. George Magoha (Vice-Chancellor), Prof. Jacob T Kaimenyi (DVC Academic Affairs), Mr Ben M Waweru (Academic Registrar), Prof. Dominic Wamugunda (Dean of Students), Mr David Osiany (Chair of SONU), Mr Nickson Korir (Secretary-General of SONU)
Network	Higher Education Research and Advocacy Network in Africa (HERANA)

Executive Summary

The context

In the past two decades, a great number of African nations embarked on a political transition from single-party authoritarianism, military rule and presidential strongman rule, towards economic and political liberalisation and democratisation, embracing competitive, multi-party electoral systems within an enabling framework of political and civil rights. Various comparative indicators of democracy and good governance indicate, however, that the democratisation of state and society in Africa is an ongoing project; democratic governance in Africa remains constrained by serious flaws. While well-designed political institutions and processes constitute the necessary 'hardware' of a democratic system, democracy requires democrats to consolidate.

Higher education is recognised as key to delivering the knowledge requirements for political development. It is essential for the design and operation of key political institutions of a modern political system, from the judiciary to the legislative and executive arms of government, the top staffing of the state bureaucracy as well as key institutions of civil society. Moreover, public higher education in democracies is typically mandated to contribute to the development of an enlightened, critically constructive citizenry.

Whether and how higher education makes a contribution to democratisation beyond producing the professionals that are necessary for developing and sustaining a modern political system has remained an unresolved question. Research conducted in the African context has produced so far ambiguous findings, ranging from a strong positive correlation between higher levels of education and democratic attitudes and behaviours to conclusions that higher levels of education only offer 'diminishing returns' for the development of democratic citizenship in Africa.

The research

Much scholarly thinking about the contribution of higher education to democracy in Africa has been normative and empirically qualitative in nature. Only with the regular rounds of Afrobarometer surveys (since 1999) have large-scale, comparative, quantitative analyses of the political attitudes and behaviours of African publics become possible. Provided that Afrobarometer surveys are representative of their national populations, the very small higher education participation rate of most African countries (hovering at 5% for sub-Saharan Africa) has meant that the country-specific samples of Africans with higher education are often too small to allow robust intra-country and inter-country group comparison. Moreover, even where such comparison is possible (e.g. in the South African sample and across 'Afrobarometerland'), the question of whether there are university-specific mechanisms or pathways by which higher education contributes to democratic attitudes and behaviours, and how these mechanisms operate and relate to politics on and off campus, cannot be explored. The Student Governance Surveys represent an attempt to address these gaps.

To understand the contribution of African universities to citizenship development, the project places at its core an extensive investigation of the political attitudes and behaviours of students and student leaders. At a general level, the question is whether African universities serve as potential 'training grounds' for democratic citizenship or whether they are merely 'hothouses' of student political activism whereby students lose their impetus once away from the university. In particular, the investigation has focused on the following research questions:

- To what extent do students demand democracy? Are they 'committed democrats'?
- What are students' perceptions of the supply of democracy in their country? Are they 'critical citizens'?
- To what extent are students cognitively engaged in politics and participating in various ways in politics on and off campus? Are they 'active citizens'?
- What are students' views on democratic consolidation and regime change in their country? Can they be considered 'transformative democrats'?

A particular focus of the study is on exploring the relationship between students' active political involvement on and off campus and students' attitudes towards democracy. Moreover, the surveys were designed so as to enable close comparison between the views of ordinary students and student leaders, between data collected from students at different universities in Africa, and between the Student Governance Surveys data and data representing the political attitudes and behaviours of African mass publics as provided by Afrobarometer (Round 4: 2008/2009). Thus, intra-group and inter-group comparisons, and cross-case and cross-country comparisons were made possible, provided that the survey instruments were specifically designed to be compatible with the Afrobarometer.

The project began with a review of the international literature on the relationship between higher education and citizenship development on the one hand, and student politics and student involvement in decision-making at African universities on the other hand. This was followed by the adaptation of Afrobarometer instruments for the purpose of the study and the selection of three universities located in three different African countries as research sites. The universities selected were: in Kenya, the University of Nairobi (UON); in South Africa, the University of Cape Town (UCT); and in Tanzania, the University of Dar es Salaam (UDSM). The three universities were not chosen for being representative of their national higher education sectors; on the contrary, it is their unique status as the oldest and arguably most prestigious universities within their respective higher educational and national contexts, and thus their potential significance in the reproduction of the social, economic and political elite of their countries, which warranted their selection for this study.

The surveys were conducted in 2009 by local research teams with students and student leaders, whereby each survey produced a weighted sample of 400 respondents, representative of the third-year undergraduate student body of each university. By stratifying the sample by faculty, representation across all faculties was ensured. In addition, interviews were conducted with key institutional managers and student leaders to gain further insight into the relevant student political and university context.

In the analysis, data from the latest round of Afrobarometer surveys (2008/2009) from Kenya, South Africa and Tanzania was added to the university-specific datasets. In this way, the students' responses could be readily compared with those of the general public and the relevant age cohorts of youths without higher education in each country.

A potential contribution of higher education to democracy?

The design of the research assumed that by studying students' political attitudes and behaviours and comparing them with those of mass publics, the contribution of higher education to citizenship development and democratisation could be investigated. In the cross-university/cross-country comparison, the influence of the respective national political contexts on students' political attitudes and behaviours can be perceived throughout the survey findings. Yet, the particularities conditioned by the macro-political context do not distract from important commonalities found among the students at the three universities, and common differences discovered between students and the non-students and mass publics in their respective countries.

This most general finding indicates that students' perceptions and experiences of politics and their related political attitudes and behaviours are not only honed by a particular national context and they are not equally evident among the respective national cohorts of youths without higher education. Moreover, they cannot be explained by analysing students' social structure and specific institutional or cultural factors. The most plausible explanation for certain student-typical commonalities must therefore be that it is higher education, the university, and distinctive features of student life, which predispose students to certain typical political attitudes and behaviours. Thus, at this most general level, the research therefore confirms in important ways the fundamental assumption that gave rise to the project. More importantly, if there is indeed something unique about higher education, the university, and student life, that conditions students' political attitudes and behaviours in distinctive ways, the conscious cultivation of certain values and practices that are conducive to more democratic political attitudes and behaviours offers the potential for higher education to uniquely contribute to citizenship development and democratisation in Africa.

Awareness of democracy

Democracy is not only theoretically a contested concept; it also means different things to different people. Thus, the surveys investigated students' awareness of the term 'democracy', their conceptions of democracy, and their views on what features of society were essential for a country to be called a democracy.

- More than nine out of ten student respondents from the three surveyed universities can provide a comprehensible and valid definition of democracy in their own words. Almost all of their definitions carry a positive connotation.
- When defining democracy in their own words, nearly half of the students (47%) define it in terms of political rights and civil freedoms; just over a third (34%) as popular participation and deliberation in politics; and less than a tenth as equality, fairness, justice, rule of law or good governance. The notion of democracy as socio-economic development or access to basic services is almost completely absent from students' definitions of democracy in their own words (1%).
- However, when prompted with a multiple choice of potentially important features of democracy, most students consider all of them as 'absolutely important' or 'important'. On closer analysis, social-democratic concerns (such as provision of basic services; equality in education) now top the preferences of important features of democracy marginally ahead of political goods such as freedom of speech or majority rule.

Preference for democracy and demand for freedom

Taking the notions of 'demand for democracy' and of 'committed democrat' as touchstones, the research investigated to what extent students prefer democracy (and related freedoms) over authoritarian regime types. The following findings have been made:

- Over two-thirds of students (69%) always prefer democracy and over 80% always reject non-democratic regime types such as one-party rule, military rule and presidential strongman rule as alternatives to democracy for the way their national government should work.
- Demand for key political and civil rights, such as free speech, press freedom and freedom of association, is high among students of all campuses (and highest at UCT), albeit not as unfettered freedoms.
- Overall, only a minority of students at UON (45%) and UDSM (36%) can be described as unreservedly committed democrats in that they always prefer democracy and reject non-democratic regime alternatives in all cases. The students from these two universities also emerge as *less* committed to democracy than their respective national age cohort of youth who have no higher education (Kenya: 55%; TZN: 43%) and the mass publics in their respective countries (Kenya: 63%; TZN: 46%). In contrast, 54% of UCT students can be considered committed democrats by this definition, which is considerably more than the South African mass public (where only 35% are fully committed to democracy) and their age peers without higher education (32%).
- There is no significant correlation between involvement in formal student leadership on campus and being a committed democrat. Moreover, the attempt to explain support for democracy among the students of the three universities in terms of social structure, institutional and cultural factors, and attitudinal and behavioural variables yields very weak and few statistically significant results.

Perceived supply of democracy and democratic consolidation

Related to the question of students' demand for democracy is the consideration to what level the present political systems of Kenya, South Africa and Tanzania actually satisfy students' political ideals. The research asked whether they consider their country a democracy and related questions as to students' perception of the freeness and fairness of elections. Analysing students' demand for democracy and perception of democratic performance, the research shows the extent to which students may be considered 'critical citizens' and 'transformative democrats' who always prefer democracy, are critical or very critical of the current extent of democracy in their country, and are impatient to see regime change.

- The majority of the students of all three universities consider their country as 'not a democracy'/'a democracy with major problems' (UON 86%, UDSM 66%, UCT 52%). Most critical are students from the University of Nairobi where less than 15% consider their country democratic.
- The students from all three universities are generally *far more critical* of the extent of democracy in their country than their age peers without higher education and the mass publics in their respective countries. While 43% of Kenyans consider their country a 'full democracy'/'democracy with minor problems' only 15% of UON students do. 74% of Tanzanians and 58% of South Africans think their country is a full or almost full democracy as against 34% of the UDSM students and 48% of the UCT students. The low democracy endorsement that Kenya receives may be understood in relation to the post-2007 election turmoil there.
- Most of the students from the two East African universities are not satisfied with the way government works in their country (UON 87%, UDSM 70%). Only at UCT is a majority of the students 'fairly' or 'very satisfied' with the way democracy works in their country (57%), which is more than South Africans in general (49%).
- Taking the notions of equilibrium/disequilibrium between demand for democracy and supply of democracy as an indicator for the extent to which an existing regime is considered as consolidated, it emerges that the Kenyan political system is unconsolidated and ready for pro-democratic regime change from a UON student perspective, while the Tanzanian regime offers some room for reform and deepening democracy from the UDSM student perspective (but less so from the perspective of Tanzanians in general). In contrast, South African democracy appears fairly consolidated in the UCT students' view.
- Correspondingly, a majority of UON students (61%) emerge as potentially transformative democrats, that is, citizens who always prefer democracy, are critical or very critical of the current extent of democracy in their country, and are impatient to see regime change. Just under half of UDSM students (47%) and about 40% of the UCT students equally qualify as pro-democratically minded potential regime transformers. The number of complacent and fairly uncritical democrats is highest among UCT students with over 32% of respondents falling into this category.
- The students from all three campuses are significantly more likely to be critical and impatient transformative democrats than their respective fellow citizens and their same age peers without higher education. (Percentage of transformative democrats

of same age cohort without higher education in the mass sample: Kenya 29%, SA 26%, TZN 29%).

Cognitive engagement, political participation and active citizenship

Democratic processes require the active participation of citizens, over and above participation in elections, in order to be sustained. The classic Kantian distinction between active and passive citizens implies that only those citizens who in one way or another actively participate in decision-making are indeed different from the subjects of a non-democratic polity (Weinrib 2008). In order for students to be able to successfully participate in politics on and off campus, they need to be cognitively engaged and aware of public affairs and politics around them. Conversely, active participation presumably also has a positive feedback into cognitive awareness of politics as citizens learn about politics while doing it. The following findings were made:

- Students are not necessarily more interested in politics than their fellow citizens in general. However, they discuss politics far more frequently than their age peers without higher education or the general public in their country. Almost all the students of all three universities (≥95%) say they discuss politics frequently or at least occasionally with their friends and family, as against three-quarters of same age youths in general in Kenya (78%) and Tanzania (75%) and 63% in South Africa.
- Students make frequent use of a diversity of news media (i.e. radio, TV, newspapers, internet) at a level equal to or above that of mass publics. While access to and use of radio is the most popular and frequently used news medium among mass publics in all three countries, the Nairobi students use radio as frequently as TV and the internet (86% use it daily or almost daily); the students in Dar es Salaam most frequently use radio (93%) and TV (92%); and Cape Town students most frequently use the internet (86% daily or almost daily use).
- Use of newspapers among UCT students (52%) is about equal to that of mass publics (54%) and their age cohort without higher education (52%). Among University of Nairobi students, newspaper use is considerably higher (72% read it daily or almost daily) than the national usage (30%). The difference is even larger in Tanzania where 79% of the University of Dar es Salaam students use newspapers almost daily as against only 23% of Tanzanians in general.
- Internet access to news is almost entirely a student privilege. While 85% or more of the students in all three universities say they have access to and use the internet daily or several times a week, only around 10% of mass publics have this kind of access. Even among the relevant age cohort without higher education, internet use is no higher than among publics in general.
- Thus, on all three campuses, access to information about public affairs and politics (and thus potential for informed cognitive engagement) is considerably better and more frequent than among the relevant publics in general and the same age peer groups without higher education in their respective countries.
- Whether the advantages for cognitive engagement provided by the university environment translate into better knowledge about politics cannot be said conclusively. The surveys show, however, that UON students are highly knowledgeable about

- political incumbents and officials on and off campus, and about features of decision-making institutions (albeit much less so), followed by UDSM and UCT students.
- Self-reported student participation in national elections is about equal to their age cohorts among UON and UCT students (79% and 62% respectively), but lower among UDSM students (62% as against 83% of the national age cohort).
- As has been found in the Afrobarometer surveys, generally a much greater percentage of respondents participate in collective political activity (meetings and protests – 39% in the student surveys) than in individual political activity (writing letters and contacting officials – only 13% of students surveyed).
- Student participation in political meetings and protests on and off campus is highest at UDSM, followed by UON and UCT. At UDSM, 50% of students have taken part in a student demonstration in the last 12 months and 36% in a national demonstration; 29% of UON students participated in a demonstration on campus and 28% off campus; and 21% of the UCT students demonstrated on campus and 17% participated in an (off-campus) national demonstration. Except for UCT students, who participate in national demonstrations about as much as South Africans in general, students at UON and UDSM are around twice as likely to demonstrate as their respective compatriots.
- Active organisational membership in non-religious voluntary associations off campus is much higher among UCT students (43%) and UDSM students (53%) than among their respective national age cohorts (SA: 11%, TZN: 29%). It is slightly higher among UON students (48%) than Kenyans of 22–25 years without higher education (43%). Active organisational membership in religious groups off campus is about the same (UCT, UDSM) and slightly less (by about 10% at UON) among students than their age cohorts without higher education.
- In addition to more prevalent active membership in off-campus secular voluntary associations, students are also highly involved in campus-based student organisations. As many as 71% of the students at UDSM, 63% at UON and 57% at UCT claim active membership or leadership in a campus-based organisation.
- Students are more likely to be leaders of off-campus voluntary organisations than their respective age cohort without higher education – 29% of UON students (vs. 12% of their Kenyan age cohort); 15% of UDSM students (vs. 1% of 22–26-year-old Tanzanians), and 13% of UCT students (vs. 4% of South African 20–23-year-olds) claim being an official leader of an off-campus secular association.
- With respect to cognitive engagement and political participation, all three universities therefore offer significant advantages to the politically interested and politically-participatory student.
- A minority of students on each campus can be described as active citizens in the sense that they always prefer democracy and either participate in protesting/demonstrations or act in formal capacities as official student leaders on campus. The active citizens represent 35% of students at UDSM, 27% at UON and 22% at UCT. However, compared to their fellow citizens in general, students are much more likely to be active democratic citizens. The disaggregation of mass data into the relevant age cohort shows that it is *not youthfulness* in general that accounts for the more activist involvement of students in politics, but predispositions and/or conditions associated with being at university.

- Students specialise politically in that they focus their political activity on a particular type of political participation. Student leaders who operate within the formal organisational context of student government and student representation also tend to take leadership in other formal organisational contexts (on and off campus); conversely, students inclined towards informal collective political activity on campus (especially protesting) also engage in such political activity off campus. Formal and informal student leadership represent different student political specialisations on all three campuses.
- Overall, the university and student life therefore present unmatched opportunities for exercising political activity and organisational leadership at a young age. Students are not only seated closer to the political action as observers but also as political actors. While the university and various aspects of student life therefore offer a potential training ground for active citizenship (both in conventional and unconventional forms of political participation), the findings are also consistent with a potential 'hothouse effect' whereby high levels of citizenship involvement might disappear once a student leaves university and loses the advantages for cognitive engagement and political participation offered by the university.

Student representation and university governance

If extra-curricular student development and student governance can serve as a training ground to instil and support democratic values and practices, to what extent do students perceive this to be the case already? What are students' views on their university, university governance and student representation in university governance?

- The majority of students of all three universities look to the university to provide them with the kind of qualification that will enable them to find quality employment and to provide them with an education of the highest international standard. They see the university first and foremost as an academic facility and a community of learning; moreover a sizeable group also concedes to a national developmental mandate for the university (most at UDSM, least at UCT).
- Correspondingly, students have a rather enlightened view of university governance. Overall students prefer the university to be governed representatively, whereby decisions about the university should be made predominantly by internal constituencies (senior management, the professoriate/academic staff and students) rather than by national government. Over 80% of students reject the suggestion that student involvement in decision-making is a waste of time; almost the same large majority supports student representation at all levels of university decision-making. Yet, even if it may present a tempting proposition, the idea that students should have '*the predominant voice and run the university responsive to student interests*' struggles to gather a majority at UON and UDSM and receives support of only one-third of the students at UCT.
- Support for representative university governance and democratic student representation comes in a context of student dissatisfaction with the way student representation actually works as well as relatively high levels of distrust in student leadership and perceptions of student leadership corruption (especially at UON and UDSM, and to a much lesser degree at UCT).

- The disjuncture between students' demand for representative university governance and democratic student representation on the one hand, and student perception of the supply of democratic student governance on the other hand, along with their displayed lack of trust and faith in student leadership, offer an opportunity for rethinking student participation in university governance.

Democracy, the university and student development: Conclusions and implications

Overall, the research shows that the potential of a university to act as a training ground for democratic citizenship is best realised by supporting students' exercise of democratic leadership on campus. This in turn develops and fosters democratic leadership in civil society. Several related findings point towards a distinct student pathway to leadership in civil society. The university's response to student political activity, student representation in university governance and other aspects of extra-curricular student life needs to be examined for ways in which African universities can instil and support democratic values and practices. In this way their potential as a democratic training ground can be realised.

In conclusion, encouraging and facilitating student leadership in various forms of on-campus political activity and in a range of student organisations is one of the most promising ways in which African universities can act as training grounds for democratic citizenship. Strengthening student development in various organisational and leadership contexts through specific training and targeted support represents a key opportunity for the African university to simultaneously enhance student life and the university's contribution to citizenship development and the development of a national democratic political culture.

The following implications for African universities can be derived from the findings and conclusions in this report:

- It is necessary to stimulate a series of dialogues between governments, institutional managers, student development professionals and student leaders on student development as a pathway to democratic citizenship development in Africa.
- In-depth investigations into democratic best practice of student development in general, and student leadership development in particular, should be conducted and the findings presented in a series of handbooks for use by student development professionals in African universities.
- The number of surveys should be extended to other African universities along with the in-depth investigations into best practices of democratic student development.
- A study of the role of youth and students in particular, and members of local universities in general in the current political transitions in West and North Africa (e.g. Ivory Coast and Egypt), should be conducted as a contribution towards a deeper understanding of the role of students in democratisation processes in Africa.

Chapter 1
HERANA Higher Education and Democracy: The Student Governance Surveys

1.1 Project overview

The Higher Education Research and Advocacy Network in Africa (HERANA) was established in 2007 and it is coordinated by the Centre for Higher Education Transformation (CHET) in Cape Town, South Africa. The research component of HERANA investigates inter alia the complex relationships between higher education and development in Africa, with a specific focus on economic development and democratisation. Alongside the research component is an advocacy strategy that aims to disseminate the findings of the research projects, better coordinate existing sources of information on higher education in Africa, develop a media strategy, and put in place a policy dialogue series that facilitates interactions between researchers, institutional leaders and decision-makers. The capacity-building component of HERANA is the Higher Education Masters in Africa (HEMA) Programme.

The Student Governance Surveys project, on which this report is based, forms part of the broader HERANA investigation into the contribution of higher education to democratisation in Africa. There are three research projects in this stream of investigation:

- **Higher education and democratic citizenship in Africa.** This project explores the role of education in general, and higher education in particular, in the attitudes of Africans towards democracy using selected Afrobarometer data.[1]
- **Higher education and national legislatures in Africa.** This project explores the ability of national university systems to supply the human capital to run the national legislatures in selected African countries. The study uses a combination of primary and secondary sources, including interviews with members of legislatures.
- **Student governance at three African universities**; that is, the University of Dar es Salaam, Tanzania, University of Nairobi, Kenya, and University of Cape Town, South Africa. This project explores the role of universities in the formation of political attitudes

---

[1] The Afrobarometer is a major empirical research programme that monitors public support for democracy in Africa by means of a series of representative public opinion surveys. The Afrobarometer data and instruments used in these HERANA studies are based on Round 3 of the Afrobarometer, which was conducted in 18 countries during 2005 and 2006 (see Afrobarometer 2010).

and democratic citizenship among students and student leaders. It uses surveys based on Afrobarometer instruments as well as Afrobarometer data.[2]

The Student Governance Surveys project examines students' attitudes towards democracy, their political behaviour, and their perceptions and conceptions of politics and governance on campus as well as in relation to national politics. A particular focus is on exploring the relationship between student political involvement (e.g. formally as student leaders/student representatives and/or as student activists) and students' attitudes towards democracy. The latter involves establishing students' conceptions of democracy; students' demand for democracy in politics on and off campus; the perceived supply of democracy and good governance on and off campus from the student perspective; and students' political knowledge and behaviour.

Key questions explored by means of the Student Governance Surveys include:

- To what extent do students demand democracy? Are they 'committed democrats'?
- What are students' perceptions of the supply of democracy in their country? Are they 'critical citizens'?
- To what extent are students interested and participate in politics on and off campus? Are they 'cognitively engaged' and 'active democratic citizens'?
- What are students' views on regime change in their country? Are they 'transformative democrats'?

The surveys are designed so as to enable comparison between the views of ordinary students and student leaders, between data collected from students at different universities in Africa and between the Student Governance Surveys data and Afrobarometer data (Round 4). Thus, intragroup and intergroup comparisons, and cross-case and cross-country comparisons are possible, provided that the survey instruments were specifically designed to be compatible with the Afrobarometer. So far, surveys have been conducted at three universities located in three different African countries.

Throughout the project process, advocacy and dissemination activities have taken place. These have included seminars at participating universities (UDSM 2009, UCT 2009), participation in student leadership training workshops and the dissemination of findings by means of presentations to student leaders and student affairs professionals (e.g. at the African Student Leaders Summit 2010) and presentations to academic and non-academic audiences (e.g. Faculty of Education Seminar, University of the Western Cape). Findings and conclusions on different concerns of the project have also been distributed via the HERANA and CHET websites, including the presentation 'Student Perceptions of Student Leadership: Involved, Responsive, Corrupt: Evidence from HERANA Higher Education and Democracy Studies' (Luescher-Mamashela 2010a).

An important component of the Student Governance Surveys has also been its training component for new higher education researchers. By means of the HEMA programme

---

[2] Afrobarometer instruments and data used in this study are mainly based on the Afrobarometer Round 4, which was conducted in 19 countries during 2008 (and one country in 2009).

(which is a Norad-sponsored partnership between CHET, the University of the Western Cape, the University of Oslo and the University of Makerere) it has been possible to support an MEd student at the University of the Western Cape to conduct the Tanzanian survey and eventually to produce a Master's dissertation.

The remainder of this chapter outlines the analytical framework, research questions, research design and instruments used for the study. The chapter concludes by providing an overview of the report as a whole.

1.2 Analytical framework of the study

The analytical point of departure for the Student Governance Survey is that higher education's role in and contribution to democratisation can be understood inter alia by investigating the political values, perceptions, attitudes and behaviours of students and student leaders. Higher education in democracies is typically tasked to contribute to the development of an informed, critical and active citizenry (WPHE 1997). Generally, the relationship between education and democracy is sometimes described as a 'virtuous circle' (Evans & Rose 2007) whereby education supports the functioning of democracy through citizenship development, while democracies, in turn, typically increase participation rates in education through their commitment to basic equalities. Yet, how exactly the 'education effect' works, and what contribution there is from the higher education level, remains far from clearly understood.

1.2.1 Levels of education, democracy and participation: a training ground?

The analytical agenda of the Student Governance Surveys presupposes a certain conception of the relationship between levels of education and democratic attitudes and behaviours. As a means to illustrate different relevant conceptions, Figure 1 (below) depicts rival hypotheses concerning the relationship between support for democracy and different levels of education in a simplified manner. Firstly, Model A represents the notion of an *additive effect* of education on support for democracy. In accordance with the work of Evans and Rose (2007), the hypothesis illustrated in Model A proposes that every additional level of education adds (more or less) equally to support for democracy.

Model B adds to Model A the notion that the interaction between increasing levels of formal education and support of democracy is positive in more than a linear sense. The essence of Model B is that each additional level of formal education interacts with political attitudes in a way of *exponentially* increasing support for democracy. It could be argued that this is the type of potentially democratising effect of formal schooling *feared* by autocratic regimes. Writing about the European context, Hoskins, D'Hombres and Campbell (2008) find that tertiary education increases the likelihood of individuals taking part in voting by 8.5% and to participate in protest activity by 27.3%.

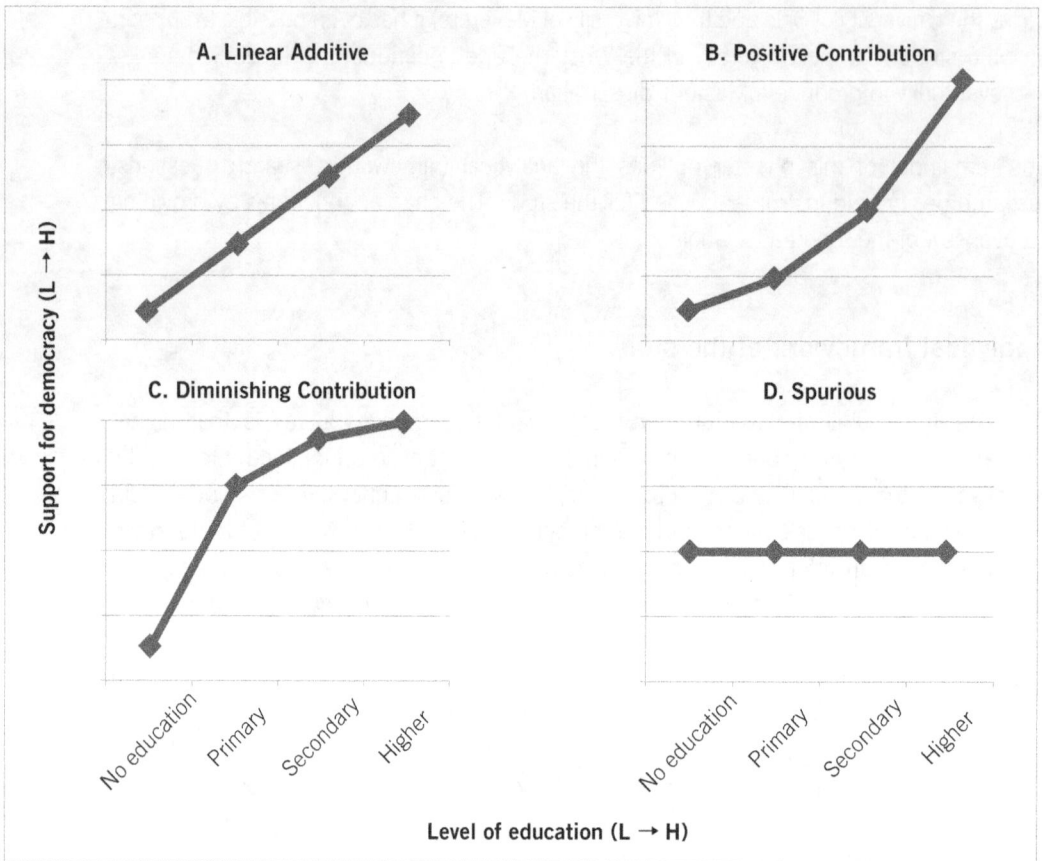

Figure 1 Rival hypotheses about education and support for democracy

Model C stands in direct contrast to Model B in that it hypothesises '*diminishing returns*' for each additional level of formal education. This model therefore illustrates in simple terms the findings and conclusions of the recent study by Mattes and Mughogho (2010) on the impacts of formal education on democratic citizenship in Africa. Lastly, all previous models are in contradistinction with Model D which is a way of illustrating the notion that levels of formal schooling have *no effect* on support for democracy; that is, that there is no empirical relationship between these two variables.

Recent studies have shown that levels of formal education have both direct and indirect, positive effects on democratic attitudes (Evans & Rose 2007; Hoskins *et al.* 2008; Mattes & Mughogho 2010). The most recent studies based on Afrobarometer data suggest, however, that this relationship is mostly indirect, mediated by use of news media (especially newspaper use), and that the interaction is such that once literacy has been achieved, additional levels of education add little (or, in the words of the authors, yield 'diminishing returns') to support of democracy (Mattes & Mughogho 2010). Model C therefore illustrates most closely the state of knowledge concerning the interaction between increasing levels of formal education and support for democracy in Africa based on data from mass public samples.

Whereas the contribution of increasing levels of formal education to democratic attitudes is a concern pursued in much of the current literature on the nexus of education and democracy in Africa, it is only one amongst the concerns of this study. The Student Governance Surveys' focus on university students has a somewhat different rationale; overall the purpose is to open up 'the black box' of the way the 'educational effect' works on citizenship development in a particular way. The project supposes that, on the one hand, university students have had the benefit of the full formal civic education curriculum offered by the education system in their particular country along with the experience of various institutional political cultures. While current literature puts much emphasis on the importance of the primary and secondary levels of education in citizenship development, higher education is regarded here as the level at which the education system's impact on students' political attitudes and behaviours cumulates and culminates. From this perspective, there is no need to make an artificial distinction between different schooling levels. On the other hand, university students are also at an age and a level of political maturity where they can be expected to engage already in 'big politics'; that is, by being members of political organisations and organisations of civil society, attending political meetings and rallies, participating in national elections and perhaps demonstrations. Student Governance Survey data of students' political attitudes and behaviours in relation to national politics and governance can be compared to those of the same age cohort of the national mass public samples of the Afrobarometer as a way of testing the different models of interaction between levels of education and support for democracy. This is therefore one of the analytical focuses of this project.

The central analytical concern of the Student Governance Surveys is to explore and try to understand students' conceptions of democracy, their attitudes towards democratic governance, their perceptions of national regime performance and satisfaction with the current political system in its own right as well as *in terms of different conceptions of citizenship* and so-called *educational pathways* to democratic citizenship. Related to that, the project explores the proposition that political involvement at university level (e.g. as student activist or formal student representative/student leader) has a 'spill-over effect' on attitudes and behaviour towards governance at national level and/or more generally on attitudes towards democracy. To put it differently: *Does active participation in student leadership at university influence support for democracy in general?* In this regard, a set of hypotheses or models equivalent to that of Figure 1 can be tested whereby levels of education are substituted by levels of political participation, with support for democracy as a dependent variable. Models A+B would thus represent the hypothesis of a positive effect of increasing political participation on support for democracy. Model C proposes that higher levels of political participation only offer 'diminishing returns' for support for democracy; and Model D represents the null hypothesis; that is, there is no empirical relationship between participation and democratic attitudes. In this regard, Models A–C represent variants of arguments in classic democratic theory (as represented by Rousseau and Mill) that political participation acts as a 'training ground' for democracy (compare Muller, Seligson & Turan 1987).

Relevant literature on the relationship between education and democratic citizenship points to a number of 'educational pathways' to democratic citizenship. It is in terms of such pathways (or mechanisms) that the Student Governance Surveys try to open up 'the black box' of the presumed 'educational effect'.

1.2.2 Educational pathways to democratic citizenship

The notion of 'democratic citizenship', the way it may be cultivated and, more especially, how it may be indicated and measured in terms of specific political attitudes and behaviours of students in general and student leaders in particular, has been central to the conceptualisation of the Student Governance Surveys. Helpful in this regard has been the study on the contribution of education to democracy by Nie, Junn and Stehlik-Barry (1996). Nie *et al.* argue that formal education operates through two distinct mechanisms or pathways in its effect on citizens' democratic attitudes and behaviours. One is through a **cognitive pathway** in that formal education enhances cognitive ability in relation to politics (e.g. knowing what democracy is; knowing relevant office holders etc). Nie *et al.* argue that formal education not only enhances people's ability to gather and process information relevant to a particular profession, but also information about government and politics, along with the ability to make sense of this information. Thus, formal education is expected to enhance the verbal proficiency of citizens with respect to understanding the political system (e.g. democracy) and weigh it against alternatives (Nie *et al.* 1996).

Another such mechanism represents a **positional pathway**, whereby formal education places individuals more centrally in society. Social network centrality is the concept proposed by Nie *et al.*, and they argue that the positional pathway operates such that 'educational attainment has a profound effect on the positions of individuals by placing them in more- or less-central network positions' (ibid.: 45) within society. Citizens who are more centrally placed in society are also more likely to be in the centre of political networks. While higher levels of educational attainment therefore enhance the centrality of citizens in political networks, lower levels of attainment conversely correlate with a more peripheral positioning.

In this conception, democracy is primarily about citizens' voices being heard; hence cognitive ability and network centrality may be considered among the key attributes of democratic citizenship. The basic argument is that the more closely citizens are seated to the 'political stage' and the more clearly they can articulate their political demands, the more likely it is that they will gain political actors' attention and be able to effectively influence politics as 'enlightened and engaged citizens'. Formal education in this view is 'primary among the factors used in assigning educational rank and seats' (ibid.: 187). Therefore, by increasing verbal proficiency and cognitive awareness of politics, formal education apparently produces more cognitively aware and 'enlightened' citizens; in addition, the positional pathway relates to the notion of 'engaged citizenship' and the sense of political efficacy.

1.2.3 Transformative citizenship and democratic consolidation

Nie *et al.*'s (1996) study focuses on citizens' attitudes and behaviours in 'old' democracies; moreover, it employs a rather elitist view of democracy. In developing country contexts where regime transitions to democracy are often incomplete, formal education may have more and different kinds of contributions to citizenship development. Regime transition involves periods of substantial change in the political system which 'set a society on a path that shapes its subsequent political development' (Munck & Leff 1997: 343). The notion of a democratic transition involves a regime change towards a more democratic society. In his classic study of regime change, O'Donnell distinguishes two phases of democratic transition. The first concerns the process of transition from the previous non-democratic regime to the installation of a new democratic government; the second phase is concerned with the consolidation of the democratic regime to the effect that there is no need to fear an autocratic regression (*in* Munck & Leff 1997).

A democratic transition does not necessarily imply that the majority of a population is democratically inclined. More often than not, populations may be merely anti-authoritarian, and democracy provides a somewhat mystical ideal of freedom, justice and equality; that is, an *ideological* means, to denounce the existing regime and formulate and legitimise opposition to authoritarianism. However, in order for a new democratic regime to be consolidated, it needs to be seen by all significant political actors and an overwhelming majority of the citizens as 'the only game in town' (Linz & Stepan 1996, in Mattes, Davids & Africa 1999: 1). It requires the development of a democratic political culture. Thus, Schmidt argues that 'regime change is completed once the rules of the new regime are accepted by the most important individual and collective actors and the new order can be accounted for as "consolidated" in the sense that its procedures and normative foundations are politically and culturally deeply entrenched' (1995: 819, *our translation*). A liberal democratic culture presupposes the widespread acceptance that (1) democracy is less a system to deal with socio-economic problems more effectively than a solution to the problem of tyranny; (2) there is a distinction between the democratic regime per se and the incumbent government; and hence that (3) democracy is an institutionalised system of governance whereby problems are dealt with by changing governments and the political leadership rather than changing regimes (Huntington 1991). More substantive, social-democratic and participatory conceptions of democratic culture will add to this procedural view the need for a sense of 'demos', a sense of common membership of a democratic community (however imagined) along with the pursuit of socio-economic equality. A good attempt at formulating the individual or micro-level long-term requirements of democratic consolidation has been made by Mattes *et al.* (1999):

> *Regardless of how well designed its political institutions and processes, a sustainable and consolidated democracy requires people who are willing to support, defend and sustain democratic practices. In other words, a democracy requires democrats; it requires citizens.* (Mattes et al. 1999: 1)

Supporting and sustaining existing political practices may, however, not be enough to bring about a stable democratic order; political practices themselves may still need to be transformed and democratised further lest 'procedures and normative foundations' of a new regime that is *not* substantially democratised may become 'politically and culturally deeply entrenched' in Schmidt's sense (1995: 819, *our translation*). Thus, the argument that 'education can change only the composition of the population that is at or near the top of the rank [of decision-making, because] the number of good seats is fixed' (Nie *et al.* 1996: 188) may be taken as inherently problematic in country contexts where defective and pseudo-democratic practices persist. In other words, not only the willingness to support, defend and sustain, but also that *to deepen and expand* democratic practices may be vital to the consolidation of a new democracy.

Transitions to democracy precisely involve that the number of seats in proximity to the social and political centre of society is expanded (along with introducing new procedures for allocating seats). In developing countries in which transitions to democracy are often still incomplete, education therefore may have an additional important effect in that it produces agitators for democracy – transformative democrats, if you will – who are critical of current regime performance and supportive of deeper democratisation and eager to see change happening. In this respect, formal education may operate through yet another distinct mechanism or pathway in its effect on democratic attitudes and behaviours – by creating demand for democracy where there was previously none or little, and conversely stimulating a more critical evaluation of current regime performance and thus the nature and extent of the supply of democracy in the country. In this view, educational institutions are seen as cultural institutions that are upstream rather than downstream of national culture. The notions of 'demand for democracy' and perception of 'supply of democracy' are important to this argument and will be elaborated on below.

In terms of the notion of educational pathways, the idea of a **transformative pathway** as a mechanism by which formal education 'activates' political demands for regime change in young citizens has been central to the conceptualisation of the Student Governance Surveys. Viewed from the perspective of such a pathway, higher levels of educational attainment are expected to enhance the disenchantment of citizens with the existing (hybrid or semi-democratic) regime by simultaneously raising levels of dissatisfaction with regime performance (i.e. negative perceptions of the supply of democracy) and increasing support for a more democratic dispensation (i.e. raising demand for democracy).

By amending Nie *et al.*'s notion of a cognitive pathway, we have thus set out to investigate the argument that transformative citizenship involves cognitive and behavioural dimensions that agitate for an expansion of the number of seats at the centre of decision-making. In this respect it is important to uphold more than a narrow elitist view of what democracy is. Rather, as a way of deepening and consolidating democracy it should be considered in its original sense as a participatory way of decision-making in which not only the 'qualified' are involved but where better decisions are reached through the counsel of the many. As Bleiklie puts it, in this idealist view, 'democracy is not only a mechanism for leadership selection, but also a form of collective decision-making that constitutes a way of life' (n.d.: 1).

1.2.4 A student leadership pathway to democracy?

The studies of Altbach (1989; 1991; 2006) and others into student activism and its causes suggest that a focus on university students in Africa to explore the notion of transformative citizenship in terms of the attitudes and behaviours of political agents may be quite apposite. The history of student political activism is one closely related to the world's major political revolutions (ranging from the French revolutions of 1789, 1830 and 1848, and the German risings of 1848 through to the student uprisings of 1968, the role of student activists in Eastern Europe in the late 1980s and the tragic Tiananmen Square Massacre of 1989); in short, authoritarian rulers have been rightly cautious to keep the lid on the liberalising and democratising potential of student movements (e.g. Altbach 1989; Luescher 2005; Munene 2003; Perkin 2006). Altbach argues, for example, that university students and academics living in the post-Cold War transitions to democracy era in Eastern Europe were the first to articulate the political discontent. While nationalism and opposition to Soviet influence were part of students' motivation, 'a desire for freedom of expression and representative government also played an important role' (Altbach 2006: 338).

Following Badat (1999) and others, the Student Governance Surveys make a conceptual distinction between the student body as a whole and the student leadership. This distinction serves as proxy of different levels of political participation at campus level. In addition, we also make the distinction between the formal and informal political involvement, whereby the former 'official student leadership' refers to elected student representatives who formally operate through conventional channels of university governance, and the latter 'student activists' who typically operate through more unconventional means of political articulation and involvement. This can include various political and non-political student organisations and groups largely outside of formal decision-making structures and/or movements that emerge ad hoc (Luescher 2005). For analytical purposes there is also a distinction in the conceptualisation of the surveys between different levels of governance; that is, the campus level of student politics and university governance and the national level of politics and off-campus civil society.

The notion of different spheres or levels of governance and political participation in relation to these distinct levels enables us to investigate the possibility of a 'participation spill-over effect' from one level to another level. The proposition in this regard is that political values, perceptions and behaviours acquired by students participating in politics at one level of governance (e.g. in formal student governance as student representatives) *are transferred to another level* (e.g. the national level, by the same students being more likely to participate politically and interact with public offices). In this respect, we propose a **student leadership pathway** to democratic citizenship whereby political values and behaviours acquired in the context of student leadership are transferred into the context of national politics *as corresponding political attitudes and behaviours* and vice versa. It is in this way that we bring the ideas of a cognitive and a positional pathway and participatory democracy together in the Student Governance Surveys.

The notions of educational pathways to democratic citizenship outlined above, and particularly the propositions of a 'student leadership pathway', illustrate the conception of citizenship development and its relationship to formal education relevant to this study. Firstly, the different mechanisms or pathways of formal education's effect on citizenship must not be confused with the notion of citizenship education. While the pathways refer to social processes inferred from observed political attitudes and behaviours of individuals, citizenship education per se can have a much narrower and programmatic meaning.

Narrowly conceived, citizenship education typically refers to specific civic education programmes. In many countries, educational curricula include subjects such as 'citizenship studies' or 'history' with explicit political education content. In contrast to that, Frazer (1998: 101) notes that 'it is also common for educationalists to emphasise the importance of pedagogical style and modes of school governance in preparing children for their roles as citizens, or subjects'. The latter involves a much broader conception of citizenship education that encompasses the ideological, pedagogical as well as political orientations and practices in educational institutions overall (e.g. Daun, Enslin, Kolouh-Westin & Plut 2002). In this respect, citizenship education at educational institutions can be said to have two distinct learning outcomes:

> *First, students need to learn **how** democracy works – through participation in student organisations and university decision-making bodies, and by developing a conceptual understanding of democracy. Second, they need to learn **that** democracy works by experiencing that they can influence events and their own living conditions through participation.* (Bleiklie n.d.: 1, original emphasis)

It is by pursuing these learning outcomes in specific education programmes, as well as in classrooms, governance, and student developmental practices, that universities have the potential to contribute to citizenship education and deepening democratisation in transitional contexts.[3]

1.2.5 Role models of citizenship

The notion of citizenship is related to the idea that as a member of a state a person has certain rights and responsibilities (Mintz, Close & Croci 2006). Moreover, the idea of citizenship is closely related to that of democracy, in that citizenship is first defined in terms of certain political rights like equality before the law, free speech, and voting rights (these are often termed 'first-generation rights') which enable citizen participation in decision-making. In the struggle for democracy in a country like South Africa, debates around democracy and citizenship focus on political rights at first but shift this focus in time. As the South African constitution and South African debates on citizenship show, the focus of the rights-based discourse may rapidly shift towards second-generation rights (that includes rights to basic services such as housing and healthcare) and third-generation citizenship rights (focused amongst others on the rights of cultural minorities) (Von Lieres & Robins 2008).

In the global South, debates on citizenship also typically involve a critique of the 'liberal' and 'state-centric' conception of citizenship (ibid.: 48). Citizenship is considered beyond the idea of an 'inactive acceptance of state-determined social and political duties and responsibilities' whereby citizens remain essentially 'subjects of the sovereign state' (48). Rather, Von Lieres and Robins argue that citizenship in the South includes 'a wide range of ideas and practices ... that may involve participation in a range of political institutions

---

[3] In this respect, the Student Governance Surveys shares certain conceptualisations and aims with the earlier *Universities as Sites of Citizenship and Civic Responsibility* project of the Council of Europe (e.g. Plantan 2002).

and relationships' (49). Thus 'citizenship is defined by highly localised processes of identification and political mobilisation and not only by the claims of the rights-bearing citizen vis-a-vis the state' (49). From this perspective, student political involvement at campus level can be considered an expression of citizenship.

For the analysis of citizenship, Ichilov (1990) proposes a comprehensive framework involving different dimensions and related conceptions of citizenship to establish a set of 'role models of citizenship in a democracy' (12). He distinguishes between:

- **different domains of citizenship**; that is, a (narrowly defined) political or state-centred domain focused on a national or local level and the more broadly defined civic/social domain which encompasses a wide range of social concerns (13–15);
- **different types of participatory orientations**. This includes firstly a distinction between:
  - an *instrumental* versus a *diffuse* orientation, whereby the former refers to political actors limiting their participation to 'task-oriented relations with other members'. Conversely a diffuse orientation towards political participation involves a view of participation and relations with other political actors *as ends in themselves* (15);
  - a *particularistic* versus a *universalistic* orientation. Particularistic here refers to an orientation towards a particular society or political community, while a universalistic orientation involves a commitment in political participation towards universal values such as freedom and equality (15–16);
  - three modes of activity i.e. *active, passive* and *inactive*. The original Kantian distinction between active and passive citizenship discriminates between '"passive" citizens who are merely protected by the law and "active" citizens who may also contribute to it' (Weinrib 2008: 1). In Ichilov's terms, active citizens are oriented towards changing the conditions under which politics occur, one who is 'active in public affairs', while passive citizens are of a 'consuming nature', for example, content with only reading newspapers (1990: 16). He distinguishes this mode from 'inactivity' or 'avoidance' by which he refers to a complete absence of action, an apathy and indifference towards political objects (16);
  - *verbal support* versus *actual behaviour* in adherence to certain principles (16); and
  - different attitudinal dimensions, distinguishing among *affective, cognitive* and *evaluative* responses of a political actor (16).
- Lastly, Ichilov also distinguishes between **different objectives and means of participation**. Key among these distinctions are those of (a) participation as a means to express *consent* or *dissent;* and (b) participation by *conventional* or *unconventional* means, whereby typical conventional means in a democracy would be elections and the like while demonstrations, sit-ins and similar protest action are considered as more unconventional (17–18).

In the conceptualisation of the Student Governance Surveys and the analysis of their results, Ichilov's different dimensions of citizenship take various operational and adapted forms. Firstly, the surveys distinguish as two key domains of participation the campus level of student politics and university governance from the national political sphere. In this regard it is important to keep in mind that the focus of the surveys is on constitutional or *regime politics* that deals with attitudes and behaviours in relation to a particular political system (i.e. the politics of 'who makes what rules when and how') rather than towards the distribution of specific resources at a specific point in time (i.e. the politics of 'who gets what when and how') (e.g. Hyden 1992).

As mentioned above, central in the surveys' conceptualisation of different participatory orientations is the distinction of involvement in **(formal) student leadership** as student representative from non-involvement, on the one hand, and an **activist political orientation** from a passive/inactive one. This conceptualisation thus combines the distinction between conventional/unconventional means of political action with those of active/passive/inactive orientation. Moreover, related to the distinction between active/passive/inactive citizenship is that of cognitive engagement. Cognitive engagement can be considered a necessary but not sufficient condition for **active citizenship** (in that it involves cognitive awareness of politics through discussing politics; reading newspapers and knowing incumbents etc. but not distinct activist behaviour) (compare Saha 2000).

Thirdly, a fundamental distinction between different types of citizens is between those that can be considered as **committed democrats** and those who cannot. The notion of 'committed democrat' defines those respondents who have a consistent and high demand for democracy. They always prefer democracy and always reject non-democratic regime alternatives (e.g. military rule; strongman rule) when offered the choice in the survey.

Lastly, Ichilov's distinction between different objectives of participation, that is, consent or dissent, is adapted to the level of regime politics in terms of respondents' attitudes towards the existing regime. Are students **critical citizens** in that they view the operations of existing political institutions critically and evaluate the existing supply of rights, rule of law, accountability, or, the supply of democracy more generally, with a certain suspicion? Are they **transformative democrats** with an orientation towards deepening and further entrenching democracy, whereby they are critical of the existing supply of democracy, support democracy, and are impatient to see change? The notion of transformative democrats thus responds at the level of political attitudes to Weinrib's (2008) challenge that to create truly democratic citizens it is necessary to remove institutional deficiencies in the developing democratic state to create the institutional conditions of universal active citizenship. Conversely, the notion of '**active citizenship**' complements that with an activist participatory tendency. The political actors required for a deepening of democracy would be considered transformative democrats in their attitudinal orientation and active citizens in their participatory orientation for the purposes of this study.

1.3 Research questions

In the light of these conceptualisations, the Student Governance Surveys are guided by a number of descriptive, comparative and explanatory research questions. Most generally, the question is: *What are the political attitudes and behaviours of students in African universities?* This question is taken a step further by *asking what these political attitudes and behaviours mean* in terms of the contribution of higher education to democracy in Africa and, quite specifically, whether student involvement in politics on or off campus contributes to the formation of democratic citizenship. The distinct research questions pursued in this report include the following:

To what extent do students demand democracy? Are they 'committed democrats'?

- Are students aware of democracy and understand the meaning of democracy?
- Do students prefer democracy above its non-democratic regime alternatives?
- Do students demand political freedom?
- What explains students' support for democracy?

What are students' perceptions of the supply of democracy in their country? Are they 'critical citizens'?

- Are students satisfied with current regime performance?
- Do students perceive the current regime as democratic?
- Do they consider national elections to be free and fair?
- How do students perceive the supply of political freedom in their country?

What are students' views on regime change in their country? Are they 'transformative democrats'?

- What are students' views on regime consolidation in their country?
- Are students prepared to give the current regime more time or do they seek regime change?

To what extent are students interested and participating in politics on and off campus? Are they 'cognitively engaged' and 'active democratic citizens'?

- What are students' views of their political role on and off campus?
- Are students interested in public affairs and do they use news media?
- Are students knowledgeable about politics?
- How do students participate formally and informally in politics on and off campus?

Throughout this report, the pursuit of these questions is interlaced with a comparative analytical perspective involving the following dimensions:

- Comparison of students' views with those of their fellow citizens in general and of their age cohort (as taken from the Afrobarometer mass public sample);
- Comparison of students' attitudes and behaviours at one university with those of students from the other universities;
- Comparison of the views of students in formal leadership positions on campus with those of ordinary students.

By means of the analytical framework and related questions outlined above, a set of survey instruments (questionnaires) has been developed, based on and adapted from the Afrobarometer tools (see Appendices 1, 2 & 3). The survey questionnaire includes questions that probe students' attitudes towards democracy and its (non-democratic) alternatives, students' attitudes towards civil society, citizenship, the rule of law, freedoms and rights, accountability and responsiveness. It explores students' attitudes with respect to their expressed *demand* for these features of the political system and also gathers students' perception of the *supply* of these regime features by the existing national political system. An equivalent set of questions relates to politics and governance at campus/university level, investigating students' attitudes and behaviours in relation to university governance issues and student politics. In addition, the surveys gather information about students' demographic and social backgrounds. The questionnaires mainly draw on questions from the Afrobarometer Round 4 questionnaire and are 'indigenised' to the country/university contexts in which the surveys are applied.

1.4 Survey design and methods

The design of the project involved conducting opinion polls with students at three premier African universities. The universities selected were: in Kenya, the University of Nairobi (UON); in South Africa, the University of Cape Town (UCT); and in Tanzania, the University of Dar es Salaam (UDSM). The three universities were not chosen for being in some important ways representative of their national higher education sectors; on the contrary, it is their status as the oldest and arguably most prestigious universities within their respective higher educational and national contexts, and thus their potential significance in the reproduction of the social, economic and political elite of their countries which warranted their selection for this study.[4]

As noted above, the student surveys were designed to be compatible with the Afrobarometer (Round 4) and have adapted the Afrobarometer questionnaire as the main research instrument. This strategy provided a tried and tested methodology and tool of established reliability and validity to conduct a political opinion poll; one which would allow an analysis of the survey data on its own terms, a comparison across the three case universities, and comparisons between the student surveys and surveys of the respective mass publics available from the Afrobarometer. In the course of 2009, research teams in Kenya, South Africa and Tanzania conducted the surveys among students on the campuses of the respective case universities.

1.4.1 Instrumentation

The student surveys were designed to be compatible with the Afrobarometer (Round 4), and adopted from the Afrobarometer questionnaire as the main research instrument. Most questions dealing with respondents' views on the economy of their country were dropped

---

[4] While the three universities were not explicitly chosen for their presumed academic excellence – whatever their claims to excellence might be or mean (*compare* Wangenge-Ouma and Langa 2009) – they all feature among the top universities in their respective countries as various international university ranking systems indicate (see chapter 2).

from the original questionnaire; most questions dealing with political attitudes and behaviours were maintained to gauge opinions regarding national politics and replicated in an equivalent set probing student attitudes towards university level politics, university governance, and student representation. This resulted in a questionnaire with 198 response items.

Test-runs and the actual administration of the questionnaire showed that it takes between 25 to 40 minutes for the questionnaire to be completed in full. Despite the length of the questionnaire, the response rate for the survey was extraordinarily high, with over 96% of questionnaire items fully answered (less than 4% missing values). The single set of questions with the highest percentage of missing values asked respondents to rank four suggestions of government priorities (in an order of most to least important). Only 83% of respondents ranked any one priority as 'least/not at all important'. Overall, only four questions received less than 90% valid responses.

The questionnaire was divided into five sections (A–E) as follows: Section A: Facts about oneself; Section B: Involvement in politics; Section C: Views on student representation and university governance; Section D: Interest and involvement in national politics and Section E: Views and assessment of politics and government in the home country (compare Appendices 1–3). The questions probe students' attitude to politics and democracy, including students' demand for democracy, rights, accountability, and responsiveness; students' perception of the supply of democracy, rule of law, rights, accountability, responsiveness; and students' attitude to democracy which included a subsection on understanding democracy, civil society organisation attitudes, attitudes towards others, identity, cognitive awareness, and political participation. A conceptual map was prepared to clearly outline the relationship between key research concepts and questionnaire items (Appendix 4).

The Student Governance Surveys' questionnaire was submitted to the Ethics Committee of the Centre for Social Science Research at the University of Cape Town for scrutiny. After a set of minor adjustments and corrections, the questionnaire was unconditionally approved by the committee.

1.4.2 Sampling

Whereas the target population for the surveys was undergraduate university students, the construction of a representative sample of students had to take into account a number of criteria:

- First, provided that the surveys sought to gauge the impact of the experience of higher education on students' political attitudes and behaviours, the duration which a student had spent at university had to be taken into account in constructing the sample. It is reasonable to assume that any impact of the experience of higher education on political attitudes and behaviours would require at least some incubation time to manifest.[5] It was therefore decided that respondents should have had at least two full years of higher education experience by the time they were surveyed.

---

[5] This proposition in itself has not been tested. It is simply one of the assumptions involved in the construction of the sample.

- Second, salient literature on student political activism makes the important observation that the political attitudes and behaviours of students differ across different faculties and disciplinary specialisations (Altbach 1989). Whether these differences are due to self-selection or an effect of discipline-specific teaching and learning, for the purpose of representativeness it requires that the sample includes, and is broadly representative of, students across all faculties.
- Third, our own interest in investigating whether there were any significant differences in the political attitudes of students who were not actively involved in leadership positions (students not in leadership/SNL) and students in formal student leadership positions (student leaders/SL) adds an additional dimension to be considered in the construction of the samples. As Altbach (1989: 8) notes, student leaders typically 'constitute a tiny minority of the student population'. The sampling procedure therefore had to be responsive to all these concerns while remaining representative of the student population and thus suitable for some degree of generalisation.

Taking these criteria into account, a sample that would target third-year undergraduate degree students, stratified by faculties, and within faculties drawing students from a random variety of disciplinary backgrounds and including a subsample of student leaders, would serve the purpose.

Ideally, a sample would be constructed by randomly selecting a pre-determined number of names from a list of all third year students. However, only at two of the three universities such lists identifying students uniquely could be obtained. Yet, even if such lists could have been obtained from all universities, contacting each individual student, setting up meetings and administering the questionnaires would have been organisationally a most daunting task, while potentially resulting in a great number of no-shows and thus in a high degree of self-selection. A uniform, operationally more feasible and more effective sampling technique needed to be chosen.

The actual sampling procedure eventually involved three stages. In the first stage, all three universities were able to supply the accurate number of the total student populations and the number of students enrolled in third year courses offered by all the universities' faculties (or colleges, in the case of the University of Nairobi). From these faculty-based lists of courses, a random sample of courses was drawn for each university. Due to the variable number of student enrolments in each faculty, in some faculties several courses were sampled while in other faculties only one or two courses were sampled. Secondly, the random sampling procedure could have included a further stage whereby only 20 students would be randomly selected within each of the sampled courses to actually complete the questionnaires. However, provided that the questionnaire was administered in class (as a concession during teaching time and often at the beginning of a class), selecting only some students while others would have to wait was an impractical way of administering the questionnaires. The questionnaires were therefore administered simultaneously to all students in a randomly sampled class. Lastly, because a purely random sample might have resulted in the number of responses from student leaders to be too small to use as a subsample (possibly N<30), student leaders were approached specifically and deliberately oversampled. In the analysis, this subsample of current and previous student leaders is therefore statistically reweighted down to (an empirically defensible) 10% of the total sample.

The sampling frame for the three surveys was therefore the respective university's 2009 undergraduate enrolment data by faculty. The sampling universe was limited to third year undergraduate students and undergraduate student leaders (in the case of the University of Nairobi and University of Dar es Salaam, excluding students from campuses other than the main campus). The sample design was a representative, random, stratified, multistage probability sample. Stratification was by faculty of enrolment (and gender, in the case of UDSM). The primary sampling units were faculty-based third year courses and respondents. Courses/classes were randomly selected from faculty lists; all respondents within a course were allowed to participate.

Most of the surveys were administered in class, simultaneously to all consenting participants, in the presence of the researchers, during regular teaching time. Only in exceptional cases were extra data collection sessions organised (mainly to reach additional formal student leaders). The sample size per university was 400 students, of which at least 10% had to be student leaders.

1.4.3 The realised sample, student leader subsample, and weighting

A total of 1 411 students completed the survey. This includes 405 students from the University of Nairobi, 606 students from the University of Cape Town, and 400 students from the University of Dar es Salaam. As intended, the realised sample represents closely the enrolment patterns at third year level at the respective universities (by faculty and gender, see next chapter). Typically the realised samples yield a margin of error of +/- 6% at a confidence level of 95%, unless otherwise indicated. Moreover, the data collection strategy also ensured that student leaders emerged as a significantly over-sampled group. Thus, of the total realised sample by university, 20% were current/previously student leaders (SL) at UON, 27% at UCT and 15% at UDSM. Using this group as a subsample for various analytical purposes is therefore feasible. Table 1 summarises the realised sample.

Table 1 Realised sample by university and SL/SNL

		Student leader?		Total
		No	Yes	
University	Nairobi	324	81	405
	Cape Town	444	162	606
	Dar es Salaam	342	58	400
Total		1 110	301	1 411

N=1 411

Provided that student leaders were deliberately oversampled, their contribution to the total sample was statistically reweighted so as to account for 10% of the total sample within each case and across the three cases. Moreover, the three university samples were statistically weighted to count 400 responses each. The weights applied to responses can be seen in Table 2.

The statistically reweighted sample is made up of 1 200 responses (N=1 200.164), which are equally distributed between the three universities at 400 responses each. Moreover, in each university, the subsample of (current and previous) student leaders now constitutes 40 responses (10% of the total sample) (compare Table 2).

Table 2 Applied weights

			Weight	N responses	N weighted responses
University	Nairobi	SNL	1.111	324	360
		SL	.494	81	40
	Cape Town	SNL	.811	444	360
		SL	.247	162	40
	Dar es Salaam	SNL	1.053	342	360
		SL	.689	58	40
Total				1 411	1 200

N unweighted=1 411; N weighted=1 200

1.4.4 Comparative Afrobarometer data

Data from the mass publics used for comparative purposes all originates from the Afrobarometer. The sources of Afrobarometer data have been the complete Round 4 database as well as published papers on the various rounds. The latter includes summary papers of trends in popular attitudes towards democracy (e.g. Afrobarometer 2009a) and Afrobarometer working papers and briefing papers (e.g. Bratton & Mattes 2009; Gyimah-Boadi & Armah Attoh 2009) as published by Afrobarometer.

Where raw data has been used and analysed specifically for the purposes of this report, the data comes from the Afrobarometer (Round 4/2008) database availed to the project. The database includes 20 country surveys, all of which are nationally representative, random, clustered and stratified probability samples. They include mass public samples from Kenya, South Africa and Tanzania. The Kenyan sample is made up of 1 104 respondents; the South African of 2 400 and the Tanzanian of 1 208 respondents. They are statistically weighted as per standard Afrobarometer within-country weights.[6]

For the purposes of comparative age cohort analysis, the age cohorts of the relevant country samples have been constructed to mirror the 10–90 percentile age cohort of the respective student sample.

- In the case of the University of Nairobi, the UON 10–90 percentile age cohort includes respondents of the ages 22–25 (295 N valid respondents). The respective age cohort of the Kenyan mass public sample includes 161 respondents. Of these, 27 have no

---

[6] All methodological aspects concerning the Afrobarometer samples are available from the Afrobarometer website. Typically, the samples yield a margin of error of +/- 3% at a confidence level of 95%.

formal schooling or incomplete primary schooling; 37 have complete primary schooling; 61 have some or complete secondary schooling; 31 have post-secondary education (not university); 4 have some or complete undergraduate university education (missing: 1). The total N valid of the Kenyan mass sample 22–25 age cohort *without higher education* used in the analyses is therefore: 157 respondents.
- In the case of the University of Cape Town, the UCT percentile 10–90 age cohort includes students of the age range of 20–23 years (327 N valid). The equivalent South African mass public age cohort includes 325 respondents. Of these, 15 have no formal schooling or incomplete primary schooling; 15 have complete primary schooling; 258 have some or complete secondary schooling; 23 have post-secondary education (not university); 13 have some or complete university education (missing: 1). The total N valid of the South African mass sample 20–23 years age cohort without higher education used for the analysis is therefore: 312 respondents.
- In the Tanzanian case, the University of Dar es Salaam percentile 10–90 age cohort is made up of students of the ages 22–26 (279 N valid respondents). The respective Afrobarometer age cohort includes 163 respondents. Their levels of schooling are as follows: no formal schooling/incomplete primary schooling: 20; complete primary schooling: 99; some or complete secondary schooling: 42; post-secondary education (not university): 0; some or complete university education: 1; (missing: 1). The total N valid of the Tanzanian mass sample 22–26 years age cohort without higher education used for the analysis is therefore: 162 respondents.

The relevant Afrobarometer mass public samples can be summarised as per Table 3.

Table 3 Relevant Afrobarometer mass samples

	AB Round 4 sample	Relevant age cohort (without university education)
Kenya	1 104	157 (ages 22–25)
South Africa	2 400	312 (ages 20–23)
Tanzania	1 208	162 (ages 22–26)

Samples weighted as per applicable Afrobarometer in-country weight.

1.5 Overview of the report

This chapter has provided a background to the Student Governance Surveys and outlined the analytical framework, research questions and research design and methods of the study. Chapter 2 outlines in brief a context for understanding some of the differences between the three countries, universities and student bodies, and describes the social characteristics of the respondents of the surveys. In chapter 3 students' demand for democracy is analysed, in chapter 4 their perception of the supply of democracy in their country and in chapter 5 the extent to which students are aware and participate in politics on and off campus. Chapter 6 concludes the report by highlighting its key findings, some of their implications and related recommendations.

Chapter 2
Background and Context: Three Countries, Universities and Student Bodies

2.1 Governance in Kenya, South Africa, and Tanzania in international comparison

Various comparative indicators of democracy and good governance indicate that there are significant differences in the political regimes of Kenya, South Africa and Tanzania. On the one hand, all three countries pertain to the African group of 'third wave democracies' (Huntington 1991). They all experienced a degree of economic and political liberalisation and democratisation in the immediate aftermath of the Cold War. On the other hand, major international indices of democracy and governance also indicate that democratic governance in all three countries retains flaws. Whereas in all three countries, significant democratic gains had been made in the 1990s, the decade of the 2000s was one of quite mixed fortunes for democracy. Only Tanzania indicates minor democratic improvement; the democratisation process stagnated in South Africa and deteriorated in the case of Kenya, especially after the fateful December 2007 presidential election. By the time the survey was conducted at the University of Nairobi, a transitional coalition government was in place and a new constitution was about to be adopted in a national referendum.

The respective levels of political liberalisation, democratisation, and good governance, of the three countries within which the Student Governance Surveys were conducted, are therefore significantly different. The Freedom House index of 2008 classifies both Kenya and Tanzania as only partly free, and neither of the two regimes qualifies as a genuine 'electoral democracy' in terms of the index' classification.[7] Both countries register identical ratings on the indices of political rights and civil liberties with ratings of 4 and 3 respectively[8] (along with countries such as Liberia and Madagascar) (Puddington 2009: 96–97). South Africa is classified by Freedom House as one of the few fully free electoral democracies in sub-Saharan Africa (along with Botswana and Ghana) and scores a rating of 2 on the political rights scale and 2 on the civil liberties scale. However, on the Economist Index of Democracy, South Africa has been listed in 2006 and 2008 as a 'flawed democracy', while Tanzania and Kenya are both judged as 'hybrid regimes' with democratic and authoritarian characteristics. Lastly, the Ibrahim Index of African Governance (IIAG) presents a similar,

---

[7] The designation of a regime as electoral democracy is based on 'a judgment about the last major national election or elections' in that country and the extent to which such election was free and fair (Puddington 2009: 94).
[8] On a range from 1–5 whereby 1 represents the most free and 7 the least free (Puddington 2009: 97).

if more nuanced, picture of governance in the three countries. The Index offers a ranking of the quality of governance in African countries focusing on the areas of Safety and Rule of Law, Participation and Human Rights, Sustainable Economic Opportunity and Human Development (IIAG 2009). As on the Freedom House Index, South Africa ranks again considerably higher than the two East African countries. South Africa is overall ranked as the 5th best governed country (behind Mauritius, Cape Verde, Seychelles and Botswana) while Tanzania is ranked 12th and Kenya 22nd of 53 ranked African countries.

Whatever the merits of global governance indices individually, collectively they indicate that there are still challenges to democracy and good governance in all three countries. Thus, for example, neither South Africa nor Tanzania have seen a peaceful transfer of executive power from one incumbent party to another since their transition to democracy in the 1990s and Kenya has experienced major post-election violence in 2007/2008 after a peaceful transfer in 2002. However, as noted in chapter 1, the true test of the solidity of democracy is not isolated events but the extent to which democratic values, norms and practices have become entrenched in political culture. The political development and history of each country and of the case university is discussed in more detail now.

2.2 Democracy in Kenya, the University of Nairobi and student politics

2.2.1 Democratisation and popular attitudes towards democracy in Kenya

Up until the end of 2007, democracy in Kenya had steadily expanded within a context of relative political stability (Lasner 2010). Kenya embarked on a gradual transition from authoritarian one-party rule to multi-party democracy in the 1990s when the ruling Kenya African National Union (KANU) under the incumbent leadership of President Daniel Arap Moi began a process of political liberalisation. Facing a divided opposition, Moi successfully won the multi-party elections of 1992 and 1997 (albeit within a context of some political intimidation and violence). In 2002 KANU lost against the National Rainbow Coalition, a coalition of opposition groupings led by Mwai Kibaki. While under Moi the political system of Kenya had become increasingly patronage-based and corrupt, Kibaki at once expanded the democratic space and promised to root out corruption, while at the same time increasingly ethnicising politics in the multi-ethnic country. Ethnic-based group violence in the competition for land and resources became more widespread under Kibaki's leadership, especially in the run-up to the 2007 elections. However, compared to its neighbours, Kenya has experienced a history of relative political stability and economic prosperity since independence in 1963. Currently the country is the economic centre of East Africa, in terms of tourism and other service industries, as well as agriculture and some manufacturing. (Afrobarometer 2009a; Lasner 2010)

The political development of Kenya took a drastic turn in the aftermath of the disputed December 2007 presidential election, when according to conservative estimates 'over 1 100 people were killed and more than 300 000 displaced during three months of sporadic ethnicised political violence, much of which appears to have been orchestrated by senior political figures' (Lasner 2010: 1). After the closely contested election, which was widely recognised as flawed, Kibaki claimed victory and was proclaimed re-elected, which sparked weeks of violence between Kenya's different ethnic and political groups. Only after intense international and local pressure, Kibaki and his rival candidates (notably the leader of the oppositional Orange Democratic Movement, Raila Odinga), signed an agreement on the formation of a coalition government in February 2008, which retained Kibaki as President and established new posts (e.g. of prime minister) for Odinga and others. With the installation of the Grand Coalition Government, political stability returned to Kenya. At the same time, it was agreed to develop a new Kenyan constitution, which was eventually approved in August 2010 in a popular referendum.

Three rounds of Afrobarometer surveys of the attitudes of Kenyans towards democracy have been conducted so far (2003; 2005; 2008) and the impact of the 2007 election crisis is clearly present in the 2008 results. On the one hand, the 2008 survey finds that with more than three quarters of Kenyans supporting democracy and rejecting authoritarian rule, demand for democracy in Kenya remains high irrespective of the country's recent political turmoil. Patience with democracy (i.e. people's willingness to give the current political system more time to deal with problems) has dropped sharply between 2003 and 2005, and support for multi-partyism has also dropped steadily since 2003 (from 75% in 2003 to 69% in 2005 and to 61% in 2008) but still retains majority support. On the other hand, popular perception of the performance of the political system in Kenya has dropped drastically between 2003 and 2008. Satisfaction with the way democracy works in Kenya is down ('fairly/very satisfied': 79% in 2003; 53% in 2005; 42% in 2008). In 2008 close to half of the people (49%) say that Kenya is 'not a democracy'/'a democracy with major problems'. Most strikingly, the rating of the free and fairness of elections has been dramatically reversed. In 2005 79% of Kenyans considered the last national election as largely 'free and fair'; in 2008 78% of Kenyans considered the last election as 'not free and fair' or 'free and fair but with major problems' (Afrobarometer 2009a).

2.2.2 The University of Nairobi, student governance and student politics

The University of Nairobi (UON) is Kenya's oldest and arguably most prestigious university, established in 1956 as the Royal Technical College in Nairobi. UON became a constituent college of the Federal University of East Africa in 1961 (together with today's Makerere University and the University of Dar es Salaam), and eventually Kenya's first university in 1970. UON claims to be 'the premier institution of higher learning in the country' (Magoha 2008), even though at least two other Kenyan institutions claim this position (Wangenge-Ouma & Langa 2010: 759). In the world ranking of African universities, the University of Nairobi ranks as the leading university of Kenya and among the top ten in East Africa (Rank 27 in Africa) (Webometrics 2010).

Originally focused on the Arts, Science and Engineering, the University of Nairobi has become a comprehensive teaching and research university with its main campus in Nairobi and several campuses outside the metropolis. It is divided into six colleges: the College of Agriculture & Veterinary Sciences (CAVS), the College of Architecture & Engineering (CAE); the College of Biological & Physical Sciences (CBPS); the College of Health Sciences (CHS); the College of Education & External Studies (CEES) and the

College of Humanities and Social Sciences (CHSS). In the 2008/2009 academic year, UON had a staff body of 4 200 (to which only Kenyans can be permanently appointed) and a student body of 36 000 students, of which 16 000 are government-subsidised students and 20 000 full fee-paying students. The number of the latter group is fast growing.

As a public university, the University of Nairobi is governed by a University Council as the supreme policy-making body and a Senate responsible for academic affairs, which comprises mainly academic office-holders (vice-chancellor, deputy vice-chancellors, college principals, deans, etc.). The vice-chancellor is the academic and administrative head of the university responsible for policy matters, planning, coordination, public relations, fund-raising and general development of the university. According to the University of Nairobi Act of 1985, the president of Kenya is the chancellor of the university or can appoint a person to act as chancellor in his place. The latter has been the case since 2003. The chancellor, in turn, appoints the vice-chancellor and deputy vice-chancellors upon advice of the Council; he also appoints the chairperson, deputy chairperson and treasurer of the Council. In the day-to-day running of the institution, the vice-chancellor is assisted by the University Management Board which also includes the deputy vice-chancellors, deans and college principals (UON 2010).

According to the university's current vice-chancellor, Professor GAO Magoha, the university leadership strives to be in 'continuous dialogue with the student leadership' which includes that the governance structures of the university allow for student representation (Magoha 2009: 6–7; also see Mwiria & Ng'ethe 2007: 63). Through the college students' organisations, students are represented in the University Council with two students (appointed by an electoral college made up of student representatives of the college students' organisations) and in the Senate with six students (whereby one student is elected by each college students' organisation). Student representation at lower levels of decision-making primarily concerns the delivery of student welfare services such as catering and accommodation. This is done through involvement in the campus-based Strategic Management Units.

Students are represented at college level on the Academic Boards of Colleges and in the halls of residence where students elect hall and floor representatives who are also represented in the SONU parliament (SONU 2010; UON 2010).

Generally speaking, the UON student body operates politically through the Student Organisation of Nairobi University (SONU); that is, the official organisation of the student body, which holds at least annually a General Meeting, constitutes a parliament of representatives of various halls, schools, faculties and colleges, and the SONU executive, which is elected in a fiercely contested annual SONU election. However, for the purposes of determining formal student representation in key governing bodies like Council, Senate and College Boards, it is not the executive of SONU but the college students' organisations which play a more prominent role (SONU 2010; UON 2010).

2.2.3 Student life, politics and activism at UON

Extra-curricular student life at the University of Nairobi is formally organised through registered student associations and clubs, the majority of which are college, faculty and department-based professional (academic discipline-related) student associations, as well as branches of internationally-oriented clubs (such as the Lions Club and UNESCO club), religious societies (especially Christian, Muslim and Hindu), self-help and ethnic/regionally-based groups, and sportsclubs. There are no formally registered branches of Kenyan political parties operating within the student body, but university politics is said to be deeply divided along party political lines, and political parties tend to informally sponsor individual students for SONU elections (e.g. by providing finances for posters and organising of off-campus meetings).

After 2002, Kenyan universities have seen an era of 'relative tranquillity' in terms of student activism, which is attributed mainly to the 'spirit of dialogue between management and the student organisation' (Mwiria & Ng'ethe 2007: 63). This era comes after a long history of student agitation for greater democracy, governance reforms and human rights, and a concomitant repression of student politics under the Kenyatta and Moi regimes. Student critics of KANU one-party and dominant party rule frequently were arrested, charged, and expelled from the university, or even forced into exile or killed. Student organisations (such as SONU) were banned for long periods of time or not allowed to be established (Nduko 2000; Klopp & Orina 2002). The liberalisation of Kenyan politics in the course of the 1990s, and particularly the transfer of power to the opposition in 2002 opened up democratic space considerably for students.

Within the context of a more favourable political dispensation at national level, student activism at the University of Nairobi has been faced with new and different challenges. In the first place, the introduction of multi-party politics involved that the oppositional role that students previously played in national politics is now played by official political parties. Moreover, Nduko (2000: 209) argues that 'the existence of college/ethnically based associations has obviously limited the students' capacity to unite and constitute themselves into a strong umbrella organisation championing their values, visions, and aspirations as both citizens and students'. Furthermore, the introduction of cost-sharing in Kenyan universities (starting with proposals in the late 1980s and early 1990s and fully implemented in the second half of the 1990s) (Wangenge-Ouma 2008), which initially sparked student riots and long periods of university closure, has had the long-term impact that 'the majority of students' focus shifted sharply from the tradition of research, study, criticism, and free socialisation at the university, to a new situation where they would act as isolated individuals, with little confidence in themselves, and concerned primarily with their own survival' (Nduko 2000: 213) Therefore, Nduko concludes 'today's students' main concern is to complete their degree and go away, no matter where to' (2000: 214). Thus, for most students the priority is to finish their degree in time without the distractions of student activism. For a minority, holding a key position in SONU can be a stepping stone into national politics, while it also offers lucrative financial benefits and the trappings of power whilst being a student.

Collegiate student life has undergone related changes in the past decade. Collective interest in student politics and student community life has been on the wane, while the introduction of student fees has widened the gap between rich and poor students and brought an individual struggle for survival to the fore. Residences tend to be overcrowded, and rather than serving as spaces for academic and social purposes, they serve as spaces of survivalist small trade. Students from well-to-do families and students with relatives in Nairobi prefer to stay off-campus. Due to a lack of student time and interest, extra-curricular collegiate life using the university's student recreational and sports facilities is said to be on the decline (Otieno 2011, personal communication).

Student opinion can be gauged from a number of university publications. On matters of students' welfare, the Students Welfare Authority produces *Dialogue* twice a year, which is a newspaper offering students a forum for commenting on matters in the halls of residence. UON's traditional student newspaper *The Anvil*, which is published as a training newspaper by the UON School of Journalism, has experienced funding problems and its production is not as regular as it used to be in the 1990s. Furthermore, the university uses its newsletter *Varsity Focus* to publish students' views and achievements on campus. Apart from that, UON students do not have other significant campus-wide student media, such as university radio or TV stations or official e-media student news publications (but plans are underway to establish a university radio in the School of Journalism). Facebook and other online networks have stepped in to fill the void to some extent.

During the post-election violence of 2007/2008, UON was closed for two months and lost a staff member and a student. The university officially welcomed the eventual peace accord and bestowed honorary degrees on the three main actors, former UN Secretary General Kofi Anan, President Kibaki and Prime Minister Odinga, at its October 2008 graduation ceremony (Magoha 2008). In the course of 2009, there appear to have been no major student political events at UON.

2.3 Democracy in South Africa, the University of Cape Town and student politics

2.3.1 Democratisation and popular political attitudes in South Africa

The new South Africa had its founding election in 1994 after decades of white minority rule, the political exclusion and repression of the black population and a struggle against the institutionalised system of racial separation and exploitation implemented during the apartheid era. The 1994 election proved a watershed event and the major liberation party, the African National Congress (ANC) under the leadership of Nelson Mandela, was inaugurated as the new ruling party. The election removed the National Party, which had ruled the country since 1948 and had instituted the apartheid system, from wielding majority power even though it retained control of one province and was included alongside other minority parties (such as the Inkatha Freedom Party) in a Government of National Unity. In every subsequent election since 1994 the ANC has increased its majority substantially, until the 2009 election in which it lost the two-thirds majority gained narrowly in 1999 (Rosenberg 2009). The South African constitution finalised in 1996 is hailed as a state-of-the-art constitution that established a system of checks and balances between the executive, legislative and judicial branches of government. It includes an extensive Bill of Rights that provides for classic political as well as a range of socio-economic rights, a number of independent watchdog agencies and commissions, and it is guarded by an independent Constitutional Court (Mattes *et al.* 1999; Rosenberg 2009).

After 15 years of ANC rule, the country's multi-party system has all the characteristics of a 'one-party dominant system' (Mintz *et al.* 2006: 214) in which none of the existing opposition parties is likely to successfully challenge the ANC's majority in the near future. On the one hand, every election since 1994 has been declared free and fair; on the other hand, in a context where the ANC retains 65.5% of the national vote and its closest contender, the Democratic Alliance (DA) merely wins 16.7%, the focus of politics and questions concerning regime stability necessarily turn increasingly towards the inside of the ruling party. In this respect it is worrisome that the latest transfer of power within the ruling party to Jacob Zuma (initiated at the 2007 ANC national conference in Polokwane) was particularly bruising. It resulted not only in the unceremonious removal of the incumbent President Thabo Mbeki from power in 2008 but also the formation of a break-away faction, led by the former defence minister and the former premier of the Gauteng province, to form a new party in the second half of 2008 (along with other Mbeki allies), just ahead of the April 2009 election (Rosenberg 2009).

Afrobarometer surveys of popular attitude towards democracy in South Africa are in their fifth round (2000; 2002; 2004; 2006; 2008). The 2008 survey finds that support for democracy in South Africa and the rejection of authoritarian alternatives remains high over time. South Africans also remain very supportive of specific democratic institutions (such as elections and parliament) and a majority endorses a role for the media to monitor government. The perceived extent of democracy in the country is continuously high; 58% of South Africans consider their country 'a democracy with minor problems'/'a full democracy' in 2008 (but it has been declining since its high-point of 67% in 2004). Satisfaction with the way democracy works has also been declining from a high-point of 67% in 2004 to 49% in 2008. Lastly, ratings of the freeness and fairness of elections and the extent of freedoms (free speech, freedom of association, voting freedom) are consistently very positive (Afrobarometer 2009b).

2.3.2 The University of Cape Town, university governance and students

Within the South African higher education system, the University of Cape Town (UCT) enjoys a privileged position. It is the oldest university of South Africa, with roots dating back to 1829, and has been a full university since 1918. It is one of the top four research universities in the country, along with the University of Pretoria, the University of Stellenbosch, and the University of the Witwatersrand (Bunting, Sheppard, Cloete & Belding 2010). Internationally, the Times Higher Education Supplement ranks the University of Cape Town as the top African university (ranked 107 in 2010 up from 146 in 2009). In the Academic Ranking of World Universities by Shanghai Jin Tao University,

UCT ranks in the 201–302 category and as the top-rated institution in Africa (ARWU 2009; also see Webometrics 2010).

UCT considers itself a 'complete' university in that it conducts teaching and research in all the traditional university disciplines, organised in the faculties of Humanities (including the social sciences, humanities and arts), Law, Sciences, Engineering, Commerce, and Health Sciences (incorporating the Medical School). The university has an international outlook and aspires to be a 'premier academic meeting point between South Africa, the rest of Africa and the world' (UCT 2010). In 2009 UCT had a student body of close to 24 000 students, of which 16 000 were undergraduate students and about 20% of the total student body were international students.

As a public university, UCT is governed autonomously by a University Council with a 60% external membership and a predominantly professorial Senate responsible for academic affairs, from which close to 100 joint-committees, committees and working groups cascade down. The vice-chancellor (appointed by the Council upon advice of Senate and the Institutional Forum after a lengthy competitive selection process) is the university's chief executive and manages its day-to-day affairs supported by deputy vice-chancellors and a senior leadership team of executive directors and executive deans (Luescher 2009).

Students are formally involved at all levels and in almost all domains of university governance as full members. The national Higher Education Act (1997), the Institutional Statute of the University (2002) and institutional rules provide for the establishment of a Students' Representative Council (SRC) and for student representation in the university's Council and Senate, the Senate Executive, the Institutional Forum, the university's Student Affairs Committee, Strategy and Planning Committee, Finance Committee and various other high-level institutional decision-making bodies. Students are represented on Faculty Boards and a system of class representation ensures a degree of student consultation at departmental and course level. Lastly, student involvement in higher education governance in South Africa also involves representation on certain national bodies such as the National Student Financial Aid Scheme Board, the Council on Higher Education, and the Higher Education Quality Committee, to which students are mandated from the national SRC federation (Luescher 2009).

2.3.3 Student life, politics and activism at UCT

Student life at UCT is vibrant. About a third of the student population is resident in one of the university's residences or affiliated houses, while a large number of day students live in close vicinity to the main campus. Over 100 student organisations cater for the academic, artistic, religious, political and other recreational interests of students. There are a number of 'development agencies' (such as SHAWCO) that organise student outreach into nearby poor neighbourhoods. Moreover, the University has a diverse and well-developed array of student media of which the fortnightly student newspaper *Varsity* is the oldest and most important (next to UCT Radio and numerous other papers and magazines).

Student politics at UCT is dominated by student political organisations of which the most significant are those representing student branches of political parties (i.e. the ANC Youth League, the Young Communist League and the Democratic Alliance Student Organisation) as well as SASCO, the South African Students Congress, which has a primary allegiance to the SA Trade Union movement (UCT 2010). Candidates nominated by these organisations as well as independent candidates annually compete in student elections for positions in key faculty councils as well as in the Student Representative Council (SRC). The SRC in turn appoints student representatives to all major university committees, but members of executive student structures in faculties and residences (e.g. House Committees) are democratically elected by the students in the respective structures. While the official student political organisations tend to dominate the formal representation of student interests through the University's SRC and the national SRC federation, there are various formal and informal student groupings that politically mobilise students on the campus around current topical issues. Student representation at UCT has changed considerably with the emergence of managerialism in South African higher education (Luescher-Mamashela 2010b). Yet, developing an engaged and empowered student leadership is among the professed goals of the University's Department of Student Affairs, and this goal is pursued inter alia with the annual competitive selection and training of emerging student leaders as well as ongoing student development activities.

Judging by coverage in the student newspaper *Varsity*, the most important student political events on the campus around the time when the Student Governance Survey was conducted at UCT (in May to August 2009) were focused on internal university issues, namely the ongoing debate about affirmative action and race in the university's student admission policy as well as student solidarity action with outsourced support staff who were demanding better salaries and working conditions. The latter was organised by the Students-Workers' Alliance and included a march on the main campus.[9] Earlier in 2009, students and staff of UCT also joined under the banner of the Social Justice Coalition in a march to Parliament to protest against corruption and demand a judicial enquiry into the controversial 'arms deal'. (The march was headed by the vice-chancellor of UCT.)[10] In addition, the 2009 national election itself (held in April 2009) and the visit of key political figures to campus to canvass students, including leader of the official opposition, DA leader Helen Zille, and the notorious ANC Youth League President, Julius Malema, caught students' attention. However, there have not been any serious or violent confrontations between student groups or students and other groups on the UCT campus for years and student politics at UCT has become a rather timid and conventional affair.

---

[9] 'Fight for Workers' Right', 31 March 2009, *Varsity* 68(4): 2; 'UCT Workers Suffering in Silence', 31 March 2009, *Varsity* 68(4): 10; 'Row over Admissions Policy', 17 March 2009, *Varsity* 68(3): 1; 'Long March to Workers' Rights', 5 May 2009, *Varsity* 68(6): 1; 'Debating Race Issues', 5 May 2009, *Varsity* 68(6): 1&3.

[10] 'SJC March to Parliament', 17 February 2009, *Varsity* 68(1): 2. 'SJC rallies to the Cause once again', 21 April 2009, *Varsity* 68(5): 3.

2.4 Democracy in Tanzania, the University of Dar es Salaam and student politics

2.4.1 Democratisation and popular political attitudes in Tanzania

Tanzania's current democratic system has its origins in a gradual process of economic and political liberalisation that started in 1985 and culminated in the multiparty general election of 1995 in which the ruling revolutionary party, *Chama Cha Mapinduzi* (CCM), retained its governing mandate. After independence in 1961 (followed by union with Zanzibar in 1964), the country adopted a one-party political system and in 1967 an African socialism-inspired policy focused on rural villagisation and economic self-help (*ujamaa*). While Tanzania has had much success in creating access to education and services and building a national identity from the numerous ethnic groups that make up its population, the country remains one of the poorest in the world (Heilman 2010).

CCM has ruled Tanzania since independence in 1961.[11] Even with the re-introduction of multiparty competition in the early 1990s, CCM continues to win elections overwhelmingly against a divided opposition on the mainland. However, political competition in Zanzibar has been fierce and even violent. Tanzania's political system can thus be described as a model case of a 'one-party dominant system' (Mintz *et al.* 2006: 214) even if this is only true for the mainland. Moreover, Heilman argues that 'while Tanzania has the trappings of an electoral democracy, there is debate over the extent to which elections are free and fair' (2010: 2), especially in Zanzibar. Internal to the ruling party there have been three peaceful handovers of power so far. Since 2006, Jakaya Kikwete is the incumbent president. After several high-level corruption scandals under his predecessor, Benjamin Mkapa, it has been among the major tasks of Kikwete's first presidential term to fight corruption in government and create the conditions for economic prosperity in the country. However, corruption continues to be a problem as wide-spread media reports indicate (Heilman 2010).

Afrobarometer surveys of Tanzanians' attitudes towards democracy have been conducted four times thus far (in 2001, 2003, 2005 and 2008).[12] The surveys indicate that there is consistently high support for representative democracy among Tanzanians, and that a vast majority rejects military rule and one-man rule (over 90%). As may be expected from Tanzania's political history, aversion towards one-party rule is less widespread; only 60% reject it explicitly as an alternative to the current system. Support for key democratic institutions such as parliament, presidential term limits, multi-partyism, etc. continues to rise above two-thirds. Popular perception of the supply of democracy through the current political system also shows a positive trend. While in 2001 only 50% of Tanzanians considered their country a 'full democracy'/'democracy with minor problems', this has risen to 74% in 2008. Satisfaction with the way democracy works in Tanzania has also increased steadily from 63% in 2001 to over 70% in 2008. Moreover, 89% of Tanzanians consider elections in their country substantially free and fair, and perception of the

---

11 The CCM was formed in a merger between two parties in 1977, that is, the ruling, mainland-based Tanzania African National Union (TANU) and the Afro-Shirazi party which was then ruling Zanzibar.
12 The results of the 2005 survey are considered as anomalies due to the way the questionnaire was administered and are excluded from this discussion (Afrobarometer 2009c).

enjoyment of key political freedoms (i.e. freedom of speech; freedom of association; voting freedom) was above 90% in 2008 (Afrobarometer 2009c).

2.4.2 The University of Dar es Salaam, university governance and students

The University of Dar es Salaam (UDSM) is Tanzania's oldest and biggest public university. It was established in 1961 as a college of the University of London, with only one faculty, that is the Faculty of Law. Two years later, the institution became a constituent college of the Federal University of East Africa (with Makerere and Nairobi). When, in 1970, the East African Authority decided to break the University of East Africa up, UDSM acquired full university status. Within the higher education system of Tanzania UDSM has special status as a parent university, having spun off other universities from former faculties and including several constituent colleges. This is within a context where Tanzanian higher education's gross enrolment ratio (GER) is extremely low (just over one percent, 1.2%, in 2005), not only in international comparison but also within its region (Kenya and Uganda's GER was at 3%). In the 2006/2007 academic year, total enrolment in Tanzanian public universities was 39 000 students of which almost half were enrolled at UDSM (ca. 18 000 students) (Mwollo-ntallima 2011; UDSM 2010).

Dar es Salaam University's vision is 'to become a reputable world-class university that is responsive to national, regional and global development needs through engagement in dynamic knowledge creation and application' (UDSM 2010). In international comparison, the University of Dar es Salaam ranks as one of the top East African universities and the best university in Tanzania. It is ranked 22nd of the top 100 universities in Africa (Webometrics 2010).

All Tanzanian public higher education institutions, though semi-autonomous, are regulated and controlled by the government through the Ministry of Education and Vocational Training and other relevant governmental ministries like the Ministry of Finance. The government allocates funds and approves budgets for universities, and appoints (and at times fires) the heads of these institutions. The appointment and firing of executives is sometimes undertaken by the government without consultation of the stakeholders. The mode of relationship between the government and these institutions is one of state control including occasional interference (Mwollo-ntallima 2011). Within this framework the University Council, of which almost half of its members are appointed by political bodies (such as National Assembly, Ministries, etc.) is vested with the powers to govern and control the University, and the Senate (which also includes government appointees along with senior academic managers) acts as the main decision-making body on academic matters (UDSM 2010).

Students of the University of Dar es Salaam are represented at various levels of decision-making through the Dar es Salam University Student Organisation (DARUSO). The University of Dar es Salaam Act No. 12 of 1970 and UDSM Charter of 2007 provide that students have members in the University Council (notably the DARUSO president and vice-president), membership in the Senate, and can appoint members to faculty level boards. There is student representation even in some 'sensitive' decision-making organs like the examination committees, which sometimes handles appeals. Student representation also extends to certain national governance organs like the Higher Education Student Loan Board. The close involvement of the state in university governance means that student leadership tends to focus on engaging directly with top level government officials and conversely, student activism tends to trigger high-level government response.

2.4.3 Student life, politics and activism at UDSM

The beautiful main campus of UDSM, Mlimani (literally: on the hill), offers some accommodation to students as well as a limited range of sports facilities and mainly university-controlled catering facilities. Sport and religious activities are encouraged apart from application to academic life and the quaint setting and peaceful atmosphere on the campus is certainly conducive to this. However, the beauty of the campus masks deep divisions and resentment among the university's student body primarily because of recent changes in student funding; there tend to be regular and confrontational student protests.

Like other institutions in the region, UDSM initiated in the mid-1990s the admission of self-funded 'private' students. Currently students are being divided into several groups that receive loans from the Students Loan Board, from 10% to as much as 100%. Thus, some students have to pay the remaining balance to the institution while others only repay the loan after completion of higher education. This situation has lead to recurring student protests and a series of university closures, since students claim that this policy does not really imply cost sharing (as eventually all the loans will have to be repaid by the graduate), that it favours students from the well-to-do families and that its administration is frequently discovered to be unfair (Mwollo-ntallima 2011).

This current situation is nurtured by UDSM's long history of student political activism which has seen successive student organisations banned from campus. DARUSO was re-established only in 1991 after years of no official student organisation and it has since played an important role in focusing student attention on the political changes in Tanzania, matters of student funding, the quality and standard of education, as well as governance and the fight against corruption within and outside the University (Mbwette & Ishumi 2000; Mkumbo 2002, in Mwollo-ntallima 2011).

Just before the Student Governance Survey was conducted in February/March 2009, the University of Dar es Salaam had re-opened from closure as a result of student protests and class boycotts. The latest protests revolved around the issue of unfair loan allocations by the higher education Student Loan Board; this demonstration came only months after the student election crisis of 2008 in which a first run of DARUSO elections for the University Students Representative Council (USRC i.e. DARUSO's parliament) had to be nullified. Students boycotted the election because USRC claimed that university management had intervened in the process of selecting candidates. The student government that had been eventually formed after the second election immediately started a campaign of protests and a class boycott which resulted, on the one hand, in the University closing for three months and on the other hand, that several student leaders in the USRC government were expelled from the university and some even criminally charged (e.g. the USRC president).

In addition, as a way of punishing DARUSO, USRC offices and its businesses (like its student-run stationary shops and cafeteria) were physically dismantled by the university administration. As is typical, the situation at UDSM also spread to almost all other public institutions in the country (Mwollo-ntallima 2011).

During data collection for the Student Governance Survey there was no proper executive student government in place and students were still dissatisfied with the situation. After students had returned to the university in early 2009, student representatives from class level to faculty level and hostel representatives were the only ones reinstated and operating, while a transitional USRC executive had been created by the administration (as provided for by the USRC constitution). There was considerable tension between the transitional student leaders and those executives who had been removed from office by the university administration and had subsequently been allowed back on campus. Ordinary students appeared to have mixed feelings about the situation, and most were not prepared to talk about it (Mwollo-ntallima 2011). The results of the survey must thus be interpreted against this background and in light of this context.

As shown above, there are important differences in the recent political developments and democratisation of Kenya, South Africa and Tanzania. The three universities at which the Student Governance Surveys were conducted provide vastly different institutional contexts for student leadership and for understanding students' political attitudes and behaviours. The next section now looks more closely at the student bodies of the three universities and social characteristics of the respondents.

2.5 Profile of the three student bodies

This section describes in detail the social characteristics of the respondents. It shows that there are various differences between the three third-year undergraduate student bodies with respect to the average age of the students, their gender, place of origin, religion and the importance they ascribe to religion and ethnicity in their lives. Furthermore, the section compares the social profiles of student leaders (SL) with those of students not in student leadership positions (SNL), indicating various aspects in which they are, and are not, fully representative of the students whom they represent.

2.5.1 Age, gender, and place of origin

The average age of the students at the three universities varies significantly, considering that only third-year students were surveyed. Students at the University of Cape Town (mean age = 21.4 years) are on average *two years younger* than the surveyed students of the University of Nairobi (mean age = 23.4 years). They, in turn, are on average almost a year younger than University of Dar es Salaam students (mean = 24.2 years) (compare Figure 2). Thus, for the age cohort analysis using Afrobarometer data, the percentile 10–90 age groups of the three universities involve different ranges. In the case of UCT the relevant age range is 20–23 year olds; UON includes 22–25 year olds; and the UDSM age cohort is 22–26 year olds (see above).

Figure 2 Students by age

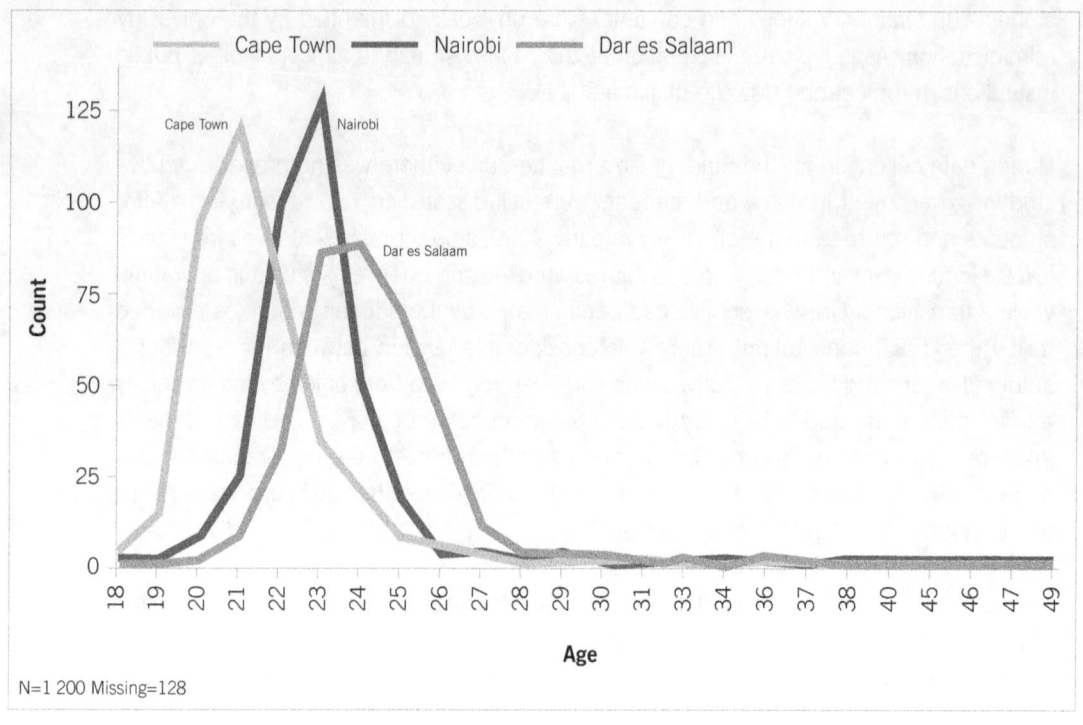

Figure 3 Students by gender and university

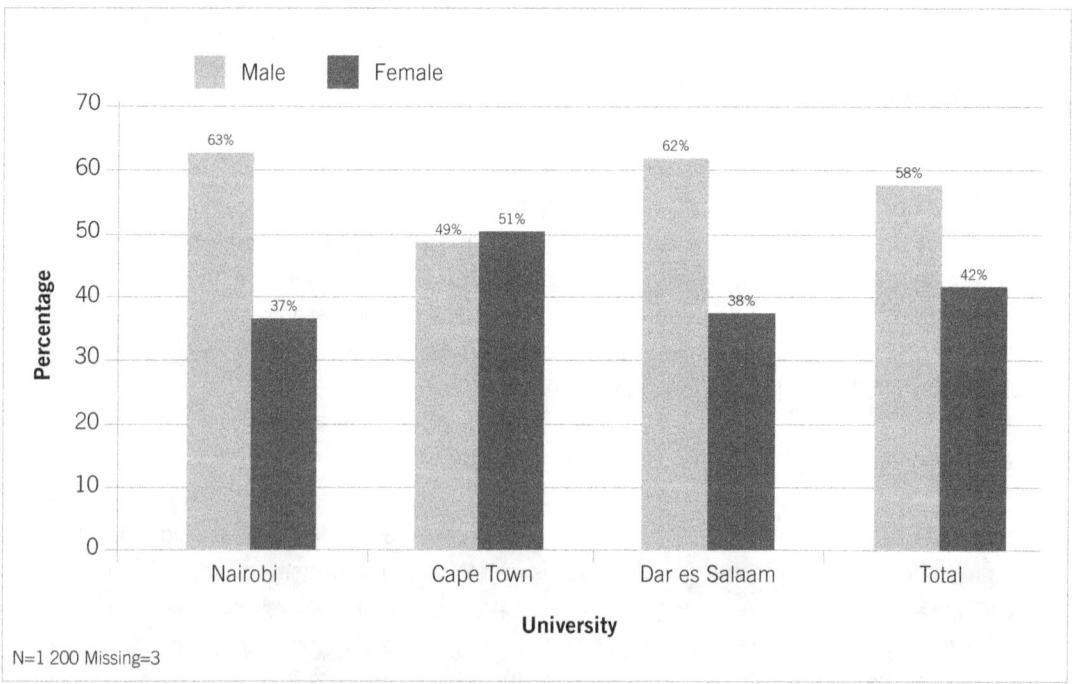

The gender distribution of surveyed students is highly skewed towards males in that overall 58% of the respondents are male as against 42% female students. The male bias originates from UON and UDSM. At the University of Cape Town the majority are female students, while at the University of Nairobi and the University of Dar es Salaam, the male population represents over 60% of students. These figures from the survey closely mirror the overall enrolment of third-year undergraduate students at the three universities and, in a closer analysis even the enrolment pattern at faculty level (Figure 3).

When looking at the gender distribution of students at faculty level, it can be seen that there are great differences in the female/male participation at all three universities. At the six colleges of the University of Nairobi, the gender distribution is highly uneven with male students constituting two-thirds of the total third-year student enrolment. As noted above, the male bias in UON enrolments is closely mirrored in the UON sample, which is made up of 63% male respondents and 37% female respondents. When examined by college it shows that female students are oversampled in the small male dominated colleges (e.g. CAE female enrolment is 14% but 27% in the sample; CAVS female enrolment is 36%, but in the sample 52%). Females are slightly under-sampled in the large Humanities College where they represent 43% of the enrolment but only 38% of the sample. Figure 4 shows the gender distribution by college at UON in the sample.

Figure 4 UON sample by college and gender

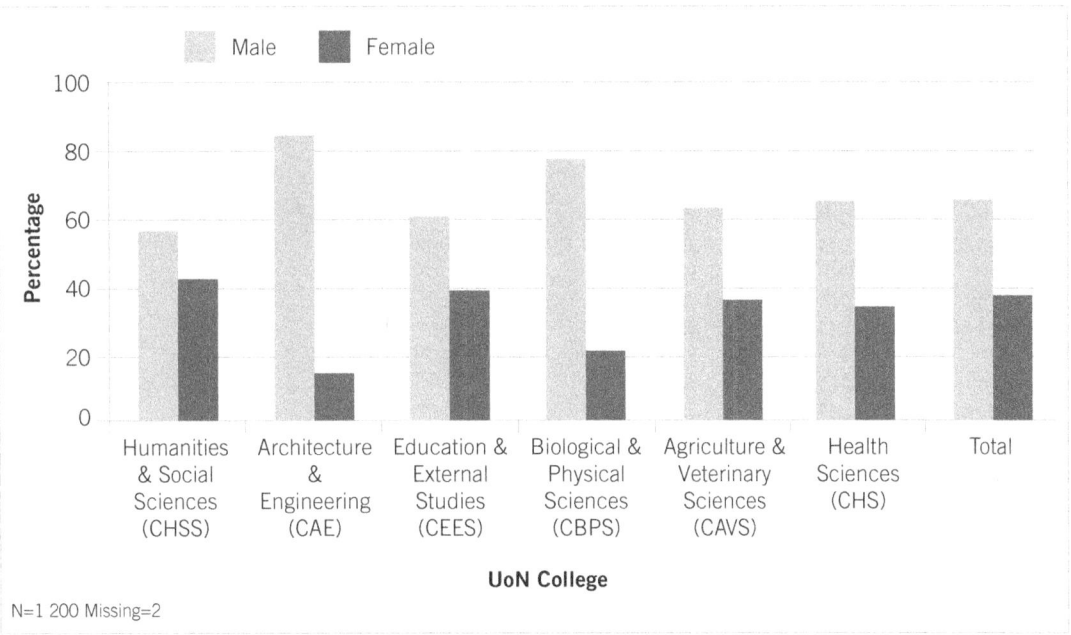

N=1 200 Missing=2

The gender distribution across the six UCT faculties is also uneven, whereby male students constitute over 75% of third-year enrolments in Engineering and the Built Environment (EBE), but little over 31% in Humanities. Overall, however, the gender of enrolments is balanced between 49% females and 51% males. The realised sample again mirrors this distribution quite closely, with males making up 49% of the sample and females 51%. When compared by faculty it shows that the samples of the two smallest faculties have

Figure 5 UCT sample by faculty and gender

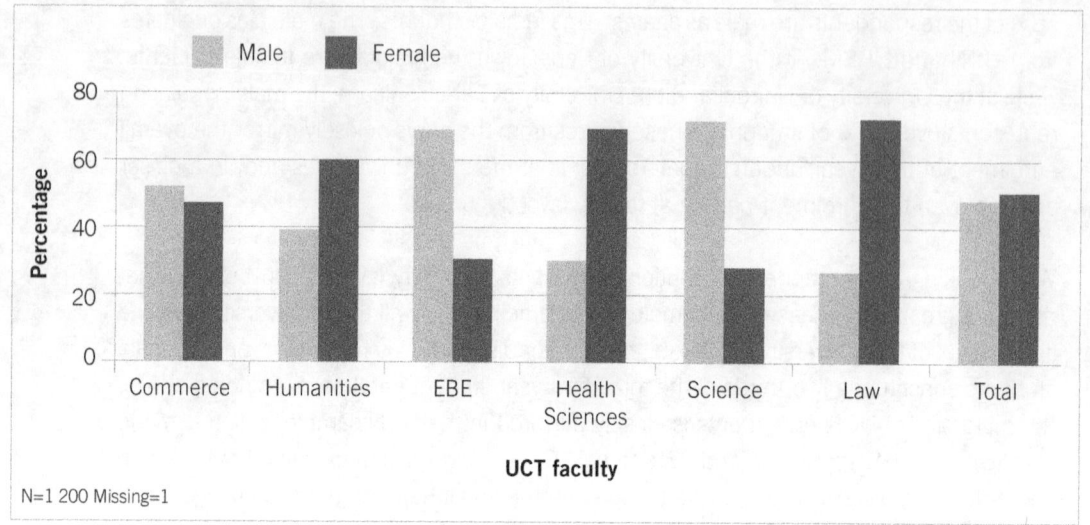

N=1 200 Missing=1

oversampled males (Sciences) and females (Law) respectively. The gender distribution in the sample (by faculty) is illustrated in Figure 5.

When considering the distribution of students by gender at the University of Dar es Salaam, it is evident that over 63% of third-year students are male and 37% female. Almost the same distribution (62% male and 38% female) can also be found in the sample. As at the other institutions, within the ten UDSM faculties the gender distribution is quite uneven. The largest faculty, FASS, has the most equal distribution with 49% male and 51% female (sample: 58% male, 42% female). In Commerce the enrolment is 68% male and 32% female (as against a weighted sample of 63% male and 37% female); the sample of the Science Faculty (80% male) is also male dominated (males constitute 84% of the sample); and in Mechanical and Chemical Engineering males make up 65% of enrolments as

Figure 6 UDSM sample by faculty and gender

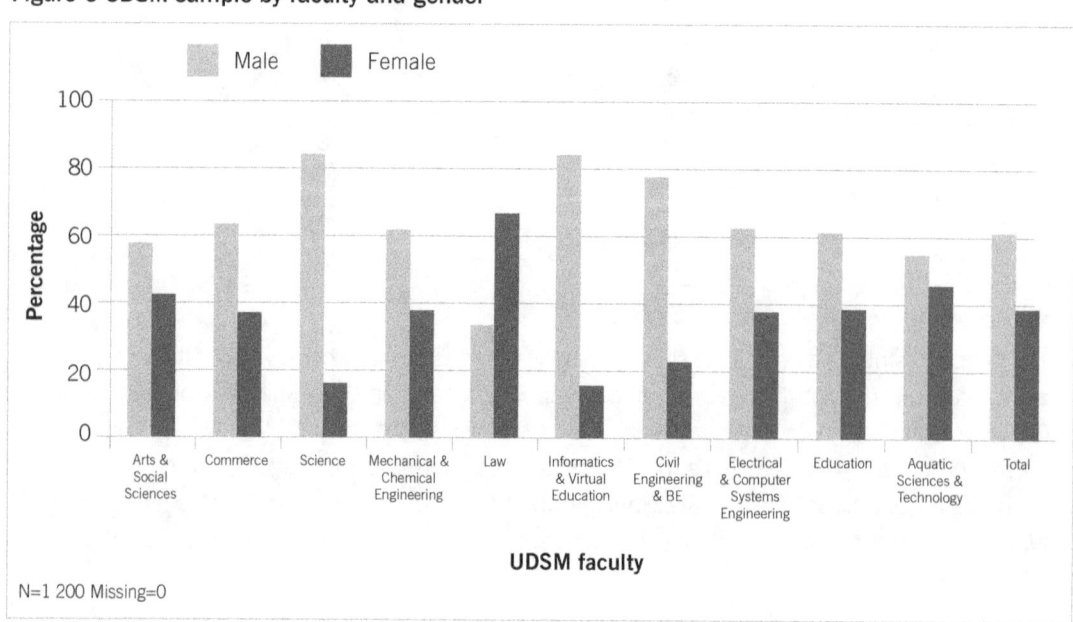

N=1 200 Missing=0

against 62% of the sample. In most of the smaller faculties women have been slightly oversampled to make up for their small numbers. The gender distribution in the UDSM sample is illustrated in Figure 6.

Lastly, Table 4 shows that overall the majority of students in the three universities originate from urban areas (59%). UCT has by far the most urbanised student body, with over 90% of students indicating that they came from an urban area before joining the university. At the University of Dar es Salaam, the number of urban and rural students is almost equal, while the majority of students at the University of Nairobi (64%) indicate rural origin.

Table 4 Place of origin prior to joining the university

		Origin (before joining the university)	
		Rural	Urban
University	Nairobi	64%	36%
	Cape Town	10%	90%
	Dar es Salaam	50%	50%

N=1 200 Missing=20

2.5.2 Source of funding

There are big differences in the respective main source of funding between the students of the three universities. These differences relate to different government funding approaches, the financial abilities of each of the universities to provide bursaries from its own budget, as well as the financial backgrounds of the students concerned.

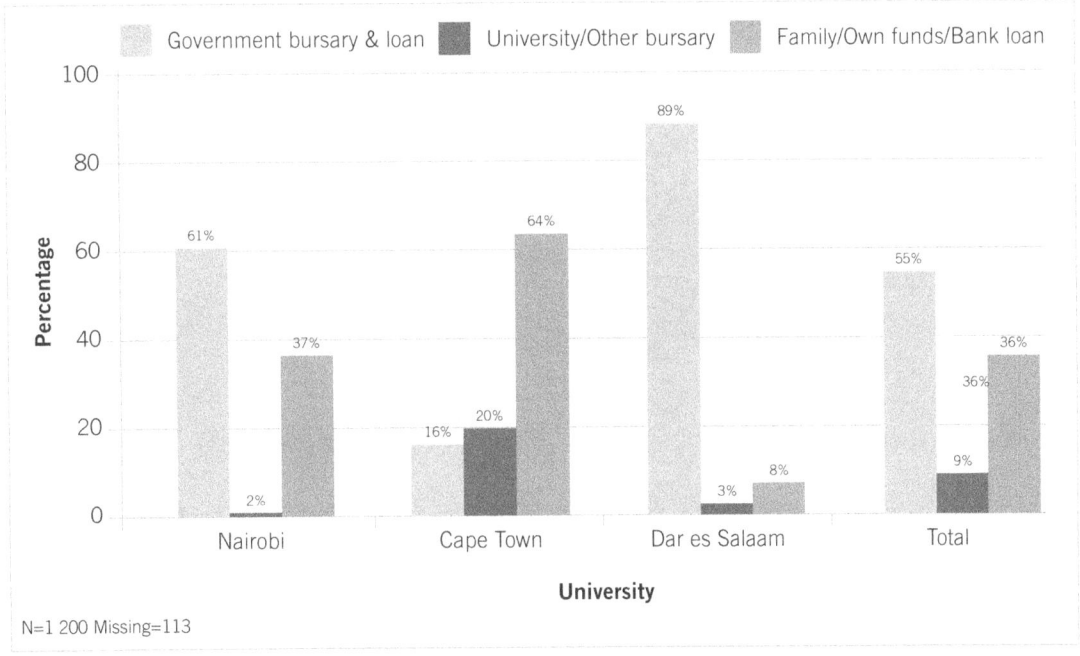

Figure 7 Students' main source of funding by university

N=1 200 Missing=113

The majority of students at UON and UDSM, but not at UCT, indicate that government bursaries/loans are the main source of funding for their studies. In all three universities, the vast majority of students who indicate government as their main source also indicated that they will need to pay back a portion of the government bursaries/loans. As Table 5 shows, a staggering 89% of the Tanzanian students are government funded, followed by 61% of students at the University of Nairobi. At both of the East African universities, the university itself or private bursaries hardly sponsor any students (compare Table 5 and Figure 7).

The figures from the East African universities are in sharp contrast to those of the University of Cape Town. At UCT, almost two-thirds of students (64%) indicate that their main source of funding is personal or family funds or a personal bank loan. Another 20% of UCT students indicate their main funding source as the university itself or a private bursary. The South African government is only indicated as the main funder by about 16% of the students (i.e. a figure which closely corresponds to the proportion of the University's undergraduate students on financial aid provided by the National Students Financial Aid Scheme) (Table 5).

Table 5 Students' main source of funding by university

		Main source of funding			Total
		Government bursary & loan	University/Other bursary	Family/Own funds/ Bank loan	
University	Nairobi	61%	2%	37%	332
	Cape Town	16%	20%	64%	375
	Dar es Salaam	89%	3%	8%	380
Total		55%	9%	36%	1 087

N=1 200 Missing=113

One of the reasons why the number of predominantly privately funded students at UON and UDSM is much smaller than at UCT is that exclusively privately funded students at the two East African universities form a distinct, parallel student body to the traditional student bodies of these universities and, especially at UON, they attend separate classes *that have not been included in the sample*. Thus, even though government loans and bursaries at all three universities are, in principle, distributed on the basis of need and merit, the usefulness of taking 'Source of funding' as proxy for class is compromised given the sampling bias in the East African samples. It is therefore also not surprising that 'Source of funding' is not statistically significant in the explanatory models for support for democracy (see following chapter).

2.5.3 Religion, nationality, race and ethnicity, and their importance to students

The great majority of students at all three universities consider religion as 'somewhat important' or 'very important' in their lives. At all three universities, the great majority of students are Christians (UON 95%, UDSM 85%, UCT 64%), of which the greater part in Nairobi and Cape Town count themselves as 'born again' Christians, or belonging to Pentecostal or other non-traditional church groups (i.e. not Roman Catholic/Coptic/

Orthodox or mainstream Protestant). The biggest non-Christian groups at UCT are Muslims (12%) and atheists and students indicating no religion (12%). Muslim students are also the second biggest group at UON (3%) and UDSM (14%) (compare Table 6).

Table 6 Religious affiliation

University	Religious affiliation – percentage of students						
	Christian	Muslim	Hindu	Jewish	Traditional African religion	Other religion, agnostic	No religion, atheist, DK
Nairobi	95%	3%	0%	0%	0%	1%	1%
Cape Town	64%	12%	3%	2%	0%	7%	12%
Dar es Salaam	85%	14%	0%	0%	0%	0%	1%
Total	82%	10%	1%	1%	0%	2%	4%

N=1 200 Missing=4

Not only does the great majority of students declare a religious affiliation (min. 88%, max. 99%), but the vast majority of those declaring a religious affiliation also consider religion 'important'/'very important' in their lives. Religion is most important to Muslim students, of whom 98% consider their religion to be 'somewhat or very important', followed by 'born again' and Pentecostal Christians (94%) and Roman Catholic/Orthodox Christians (93%). Moreover, in the cross-university comparison, overall 97% of UDSM students consider religion 'somewhat important or very important', followed by 94% of students at UON and 73% of students at UCT (see Figure 8).

Figure 8 Importance of religion

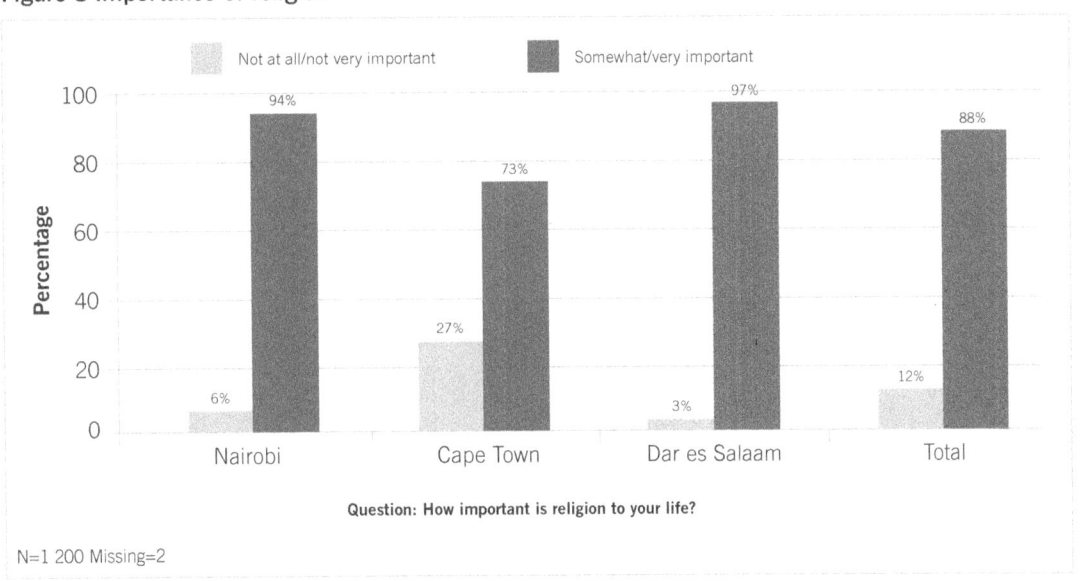

N=1 200 Missing=2

In terms of nationality, all the surveyed students are citizens of an African country. Especially at UCT the original sample included a sizable proportion of international students from outside of Africa, particularly from the USA, EU and East Asia. While their presence and political attitudes will have an influence on local African students, it was felt that they should not be included in the analysis informing this report, but could be analysed at a later point. Even after this, the UCT sample still sports a number of non-South Africans. In total 332 respondents are South African citizens, while the remaining 68 hail from different parts of the continent. The UON and UDSM samples were far less international. The final UON sample is made up of 387 Kenyans and the UDSM sample is made up of 397 Tanzanian students (with the rest from other African countries/missing nationality).

Table 7 Sample by race

	Black/African	Asian/Indian	White/European	Coloured	N/A, DK	Total
Nairobi	219	6	2	1	57	285
Cape Town	117	38	133	58	50	396
Dar es Salaam	364	4	0	6	11	385

N=1 200 Missing=133

With regard to race, the analysis of the sample is only sensible, for obvious reasons, within the South African context (even though the race question was asked in all three surveys). The problematic nature of the question is also indicated by the great number of missing responses, DK and N/A responses (especially in the UON sample) (compare Table 7). As far as the UCT sample is concerned it indicates that 34% of the respondents consider themselves White; 30% Black African; 15% Coloured and 10% Indian/Asian, while about 13% refuse to answer the question or indicate they don't know. When comparing the UCT sample to its undergraduate profiles it shows that Black Africans have been oversampled (by about 4 percentage points).

Lastly, as Figure 9 shows, their ethnic or language group is 'somewhat/very important' for the majority of students on all three campuses. Ethnic salience is strongest at the University of Dar es Salaam where 81% of students indicate that their ethnic/language group is

Figure 9 Importance of ethnic/language group

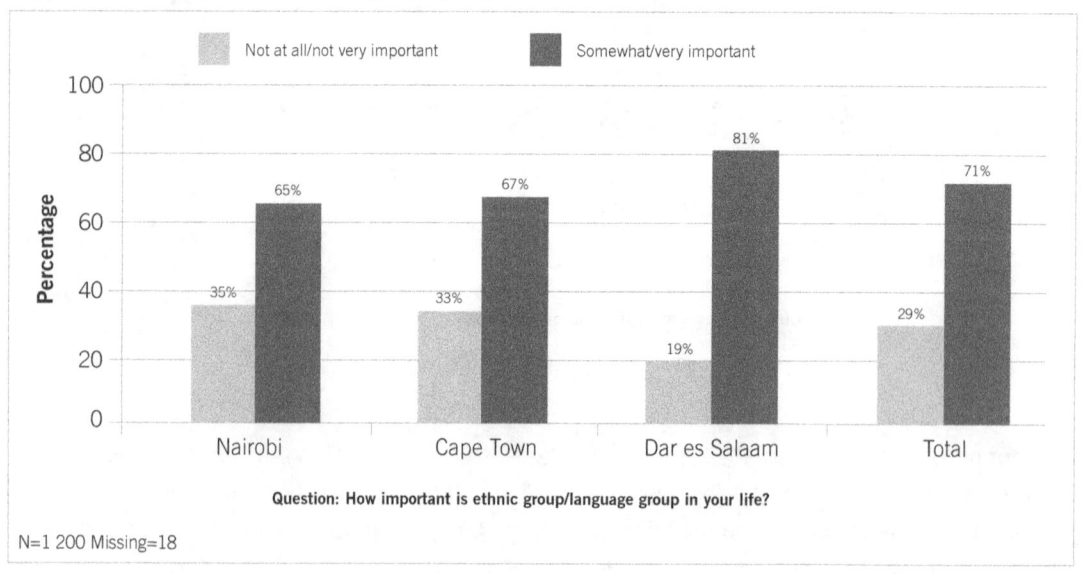

Question: How important is ethnic group/language group in your life?

N=1 200 Missing=18

'somewhat/very important'. At UON and UCT close to two-thirds of the students consider their ethnic affiliation as important (compare Figure 9).

2.5.4 Student bodies and student leadership

As noted previously, the sampling for the Student Governance Surveys distinguished between students previously or currently in formal leadership positions (i.e. student leaders/SL) from other students (SNL). The definition of the former includes students who have acted as student representatives at faculty level or in a student residence; members of the university's student parliament; executive members of the student government (e.g. SRC) as well as student representatives in key university governing bodies, like the university's Senate, the University Council or any other influential university committee such as the Student Affairs Committee. The samples have been statistically weighted to give formal student leaders a weight of 10% of the student body in each of the three samples.

The sociological profiles of the formal student leadership are described in the following tables. Table 8 lists aspects of the demographic and social profile of current and former student leaders at the University of Nairobi and compares them with the profiles of SNL. It shows that SL tend to be more often male, of urban origin, and government-funded than SNL. Student leaders are on average a half-year younger; they are more often Dholuo-speaking than SNL (33% as against 15%), while the greatest language group in the SNL body are Gikuyu speakers (29%). Lastly, SL more frequently study in the Humanities than SNL.

Table 8 Sociological profile of formal student leaders at UON

University of Nairobi	Student leader?	
	No	Yes
Gender: Male	62%	72%
Origin: Urban	35%	45%
Age: Mean	23.4 y	22.9 y
Home language: Gikuyu / Dholuo	29% / 15%	18% / 33%
Faculty cluster: Humanities	37%	43%
Main source of funding: Government	50%	60%

N valid gender=395; origin=387; age=349; home language=400; faculty=399; funding=397

At UCT, student leaders are broadly representative of the students whom they represent in terms of gender. However, student leaders at UCT are far more often Black African (59%) than the racial composition of those they represent would suggest (compare above). SL also tend to be on average almost a half-year older than SNL, and are marginally more frequently of rural origin and on government scholarships (both of which also correlate more with being Black African) (see Table 9).

Table 9 Sociological profile of formal student leaders at UCT

University of Cape Town	Student leader?	
	No	Yes
Gender: Male	49%	48%
Origin: Urban	91%	85%
Age: Mean	21.4 y	21.8 y
Race: African / White	26% / 35%	59% / 18%
Faculty cluster: Humanities	31%	37%
Main source of funding: Government	15%	18%

N valid gender=400; origin=396; age=380 ; faculty=399; race=396; funding=395

Table 10 shows that student leaders at UDSM are more often male and of rural origin than those they represent, and a half-year older. There are also proportionally more SL who study in the Humanities than the other two faculty clusters (i.e. SET and Commerce). While the greatest proportion of SNL indicate as their home language Kiswahili (41%), only 20% of student leaders do so; the majority of student leaders indicate another Tanzanian language as their home language (especially Chaga 11%, Sukuma 9% and Bena 7%).

Table 10 Sociological profile of formal student leaders at UDSM

University of Dar es Salaam	Student leader?	
	No	Yes
Gender: Male	60%	78%
Origin: Urban	52%	40%
Age: Mean	24.2 y	24.7 y
Home language: Kiswahili	41%	23%
Faculty cluster: Humanities	37%	42%
Main source of funding: Government	85%	88%

N valid gender=400; origin=397; age=343; home language=400; faculty=400; funding=395

The sociological profiles in the above tables indicate a number of small commonalities presumably identifiable across all the three campuses. However, correlations run across all campuses for gender, urbanity, age, faculty, and funding (by SL/SNL) have produced *no statistically significant results.*

Against the background of the historical development of democracy in Kenya, Tanzania and South Africa, the different contexts presented by the three case universities and their respective governance arrangements, student politics, and student bodies, the analysis now turns to the political understanding, views, attitudes and behaviours of the students, which is after all the key concern of the Student Governance Surveys.

Chapter 3
Students' Demand for Democracy and Freedom

3.1 Introduction

A stable democratic regime does not only require well-designed and functioning political institutions and processes to be sustainable and consolidated; it requires democrats (Mattes *et al.* 1999). This chapter reports on the findings of the surveys at the University of Cape Town, the University of Dar es Salaam and the University of Nairobi with respect to the question whether the students of these universities demand democracy and whether they prefer democracy above other forms of governing their country. The overall question is whether the upcoming young and highly educated citizenry of the countries represented by these students demands democracy to an extent that they may be considered 'committed democrats'.

The chapter starts by considering students' awareness and understanding of the term 'democracy', their conceptions of 'democracy', their demand for democracy (i.e. preferring democracy over its non-democratic alternatives), and their demand for political rights. It shows that students are well aware of democracy and its features, and that around two-thirds of students at all three universities (most at UCT, least at UDSM) prefer democracy over other ways of governing their country. Moreover, a large majority of students (typically over 80%) reject all authoritarian regime types offered to them as alternatives to democracy. In conclusion the chapter shows, however, that only at one of the three universities can the majority of students be considered 'committed democrats' in terms of the definition proposed in chapter 1. Furthermore, considering the student surveys in relation to mass public data it shows that the students of the East African universities are considerably less committed to democracy than their age peers without higher education (HE) and even less committed than the Kenyan and Tanzanian mass publics. In contrast, the proportion of UCT students who qualify as committed democrats is much higher than that of the South African reference groups. Lastly, the analysis finds that student leadership and student activism have little, uneven and statistically insignificant impact on students' commitment to democracy.

3.2 Awareness of 'democracy'

Democracy is not only theoretically a contested concept; it also means different things to different people. The Student Governance Surveys asked students to provide up to three different definitions of 'democracy' in their own words by asking: '*What do you understand by the word "democracy"? Please provide up to three different ways in which you understand "democracy".*' The responses were eventually analysed and coded in three ways.

The first analysis simply notes whether a respondent provided at least one comprehensible answer, without actually enquiring into the content or validity of the definitions provided. In a second step, the content of the actual responses is analysed further and categorised in normative terms (whether a definition has positive or negative connotation) and, in a third step, the responses are analysed in theoretical terms.

3.2.1 Ability to define 'democracy'

With respect to the first concern, the survey finds that the great majority of respondents across all three universities (93.7%) are able to supply at least one comprehensible and valid response. Students at UCT (96%) and UDSM (95.5%) were slightly more willing/able to provide a definition of democracy than students at UON (89.5%).[13] Between student leaders (SL) and students not in leadership (SNL), the variation was even smaller. Actually, slightly *less* SL (91.7%) provided a valid first definition than SNL (93.8%). Overall only about 7% of respondents were either unwilling or unable to say what democracy means. It is notable that almost a fifth of students provided a standard definition as their first response especially the familiar definition of democracy as '*government by the people, for the people, of the people*'.

3.2.2 Positive and negative connotations

When analysing the content of the responses from a normative perspective, it is evident that almost all the students provide definitions of democracy that carry a *positive* connotation (98.5%), implying that democracy is a good thing. Most prevalent are positive conceptions of democracy associated with political rights and freedoms, popular participation in government, equality, fairness, justice and good governance. In contrast, there are less than 1% of *neutral* conceptions of democracy (e.g. democracy as 'a political system'), and even less (barely half a percentage) of responses carrying a *negative* connotation.[14] Only five responses involve a negative connotation, implying that democracy is a bad thing. For example, one student decried democracy as an 'imperialism ideology', another as 'just a meaningless statement' (compare Table 11 below). Students' views (by connotation and university) are also summarised in Figure 10 below.

3.2.3 Students' own understandings of democracy

The open nature of the question '*What do you understand by the word "democracy"?*' is meant to encourage students to conceptualise democracy in their own words and thus to provide a picture of the distinctive meanings that democracy carries among the students

---

13 Variation between countries was weakly significant (Spearman's rho 0.094**, significant at .001). All figures from weighted responses. N=1 200; Missing=0.
14 N=1 200 Missing (no response, don't know, not comprehensible)=80.

without imposing a particular framework or multiple choice of standard responses. The variety of student responses has been categorised post hoc in both normative and theoretical terms. The full set of responses across the three campuses is provided in Table 11 (below).

Table 11 Students' understandings of democracy

POSITIVE MEANINGS	Freq.	%	POSITIVE MEANINGS (cont.)	Freq.	%
Political Rights and Civil Freedoms		47	Socio-economic Development		1
Freedom of speech	126	11	Benefits to citizens	2	<1
Free and fair elections	83	7	Equal access to services	2	<1
Freedom (general)	67	6	Improving living conditions	1	<1
Majority rule	55	5	Other (e.g. education)	2	<1
The right to vote	53	4			
Electoral choice	50	4	**Good Governance**		3
Freedom to make decisions	43	4	Rule of law	22	2
Political freedoms	43	4	Good governance	6	<1
People elect govt	19	2	Transparency and accountability	6	<1
Guaranteed human rights	12	1	Effective and efficient govt	2	<1
Multiparty system	9	<1	Other (e.g. constitution)	3	<1
Majority rule and minority rights	6	<1			
			Other Positive Meanings		1
Popular Part. and Deliberation		34	Friendly leadership, leadership	2	<1
Govt by, for, of the people	237	20	Opposite of dictatorship	1	<1
Popular part. in decision-making	60	5	It is very important	1	<1
Popular voice in political affairs	38	3	Other positive meanings	8	<1
People's power	35	3			
Representation	18	2	**NEUTRAL MEANINGS**		1
People-centred govt	8	<1	A political system	7	<1
Listening to the people	5	<1	Other neutral meanings	3	<1
People interact openly with govt	2	<1			
Deliberation and discussion	2	<1	**NEGATIVE MEANINGS**		<1
			It is just a statement	1	<1
Equality, Fairness and Justice		6	Imperialism ideology	1	<1
Equality	32	3	Other negative meanings	3	<1
Freedom and equality	18	2			
Political equality	13	1	**DON'T KNOW, NO ANSWER**		7
Fairness and justice etc.	11	<1	No response (missing)	81	7
			I don't understand	1	<1

Frequency and percentage of first responses to the question: 'What do you understand by the word "democracy"? Please provide up to three different ways in which you understand "democracy".'
N=1 200 Missing=0

As Table 11 shows, most student responses (47%) involve a fairly liberal conception of democracy as a set of civil liberties, political rights, and related political (especially electoral) processes. The second biggest group of student responses sees democracy in terms of popular participation, deliberation and responsiveness to popular demands

(34%). The vast majority in the second group actually provide the standard definition of democracy mentioned above (i.e. democracy as '*government by the people, for the people, of the people*'). Democracy as a form of government involving aspects of good governance (e.g. rule of law, transparency) makes up most of the remaining positive conceptions of democracy provided by students.

More substantive (rather than procedural) conceptions of democracy focused on equality are surprisingly scarce among the responses. Only just over 6% of students understand democracy in terms of substantive political goods such as equality, fairness and justice. Even fewer (<1%) understand it in terms of the provision of substantive socio-economic goods, for example as an improvement in people's access to basic services or economic benefits.

The surveys thus reveal that the students hold surprisingly *procedural* understandings of democracy, seeing democracy predominantly as a *political system of rules*. Whereas one large group of students emphasises popular participation in decision-making (34%), another group views democracy first as a set of political rights, freedoms and multi-party elections (47% of respondents). Implicit in these views is also that democracy is a good thing (as noted above); or at least, the responses do not imply a view of democracy as something bad. For the purposes of the analyses that follow, these findings also mean that the vast majority of students in the survey can be trusted to have a fairly good understanding of what democracy is and is not. These findings are also confirmed in other survey questions.

Table 12 Students' understandings of democracy by university

Conception of democracy	University			% of total
	Nairobi	Cape Town	Dar es Salaam	
Political rights and civil freedoms	55%	51%	36%	47%
Popular participation and deliberation	23%	25%	54%	34%
Equality, fairness and justice	4%	15%	1%	6%
Good governance	4%	2%	5%	3%
Socio-economic development	1%	-	-	1%
Other positive conceptions	1%	2%	-	1%
Neutral conceptions	1%	1%	-	1%
Negative conceptions	-	1%	1%	1%
Don't know, no answer	13%	4%	4%	7%

N=1 200

The analysis of student responses by university reveals some significant differences of emphasis (see Table 12 and Figure 10). The majority of students from the University of Nairobi (55%) define democracy as political rights and freedoms, followed by 23% who define it in terms of popular participation and deliberation. At the University of Cape Town, the distribution is similar to the University of Nairobi, whereby a majority of students define democracy as political rights and freedoms (51%), followed by a second sizable group that defines it mostly in participatory and deliberative terms (25%). In addition, there are 15% of UCT students who define democracy in terms of equality, fairness and justice. It can be argued that this latter group of students from UCT that equate democracy with 'equality' (and to a lesser extent fairness and justice) are reflective of the country's historical experience where the 1994 democratic watershed also introduced political equality. With only 4% at UON and 1% at UDSM defining democracy in these terms, there is clearly a difference of emphasis evident among the South African students surveyed. In contrast, the emphasis of responses by students from UDSM is distinctly on a participatory and deliberative conception of democracy (54% of respondents). Democracy as political rights and freedoms is only the first choice of a third of UDSM students.

Among the Kenyan and South African students, a more liberal conception of democracy is therefore prevalent than among Tanzanians, who express more participatory understandings of democracy. While over half of the students at UDSM conceive of democracy in participatory terms, at UON and UCT only about a quarter do so. Conversely, over half of respondents at UON (55%) and UCT (51%) name in their first response the rights and freedoms typically associated with liberal democracy; at UDSM only just over a third of students do so. Clearly, some variation in the student responses between the campuses may be explained by looking at national political trajectories. For instance, while the notion of democracy as 'majority rule' (>5% overall) is largely absent in the Tanzanian responses, it derives mostly from responses from Kenyan students (9%) and South African students (6%). Conversely, the notion of democracy as a system enshrining equality is largely distinct to the South Africans, for the reasons motivated above. The variations in the student responses can be seen graphically illustrated in Figure 10.[15]

3.2.4 Essential components of democracy

Another way of considering students' understanding of democracy is to ask them what features are essential for a country to be called a 'democracy'. Here, the survey provides a list of elements of classic liberal democracy (i.e. 'majority rule'; 'freedom of speech'; 'regular elections'; 'multi-party elections') and a number of more substantive potential features of democracy associated, for instance, with social democracy (i.e. 'shelter', 'food and water for all'; 'jobs for everyone'; 'equality in education'; 'a small income gap between rich and poor'). Thus, unlike in the previous question, where students were given an open-ended question, here students are provided with a multiple choice of potential features of democracy.

When analysing students' responses to the question, two main observations can be made. Firstly, when confronted with a 'wish list of democracy goodies', the vast majority of students (around 80%) seem happy to consider *all of them* as 'absolutely essential' or at least 'somewhat important' for a country to be called a democracy. Despite what appears here as limited discernment, there is, however, some variation in the extent of support for the individual features offered. The highest mean scores are received by 'basic necessities for everyone' (mean=2.58) and 'equality in education' (mean=2.56). This surprising *preference for socio-economic goods* is followed only in third and fourth place by distinct

---

15 Unfortunately, Round 4 of the Afrobarometer did not include this question and the responses in the Student Governance Surveys can therefore not be compared to those of the public in general.

Figure 10 Students' understandings of democracy by university

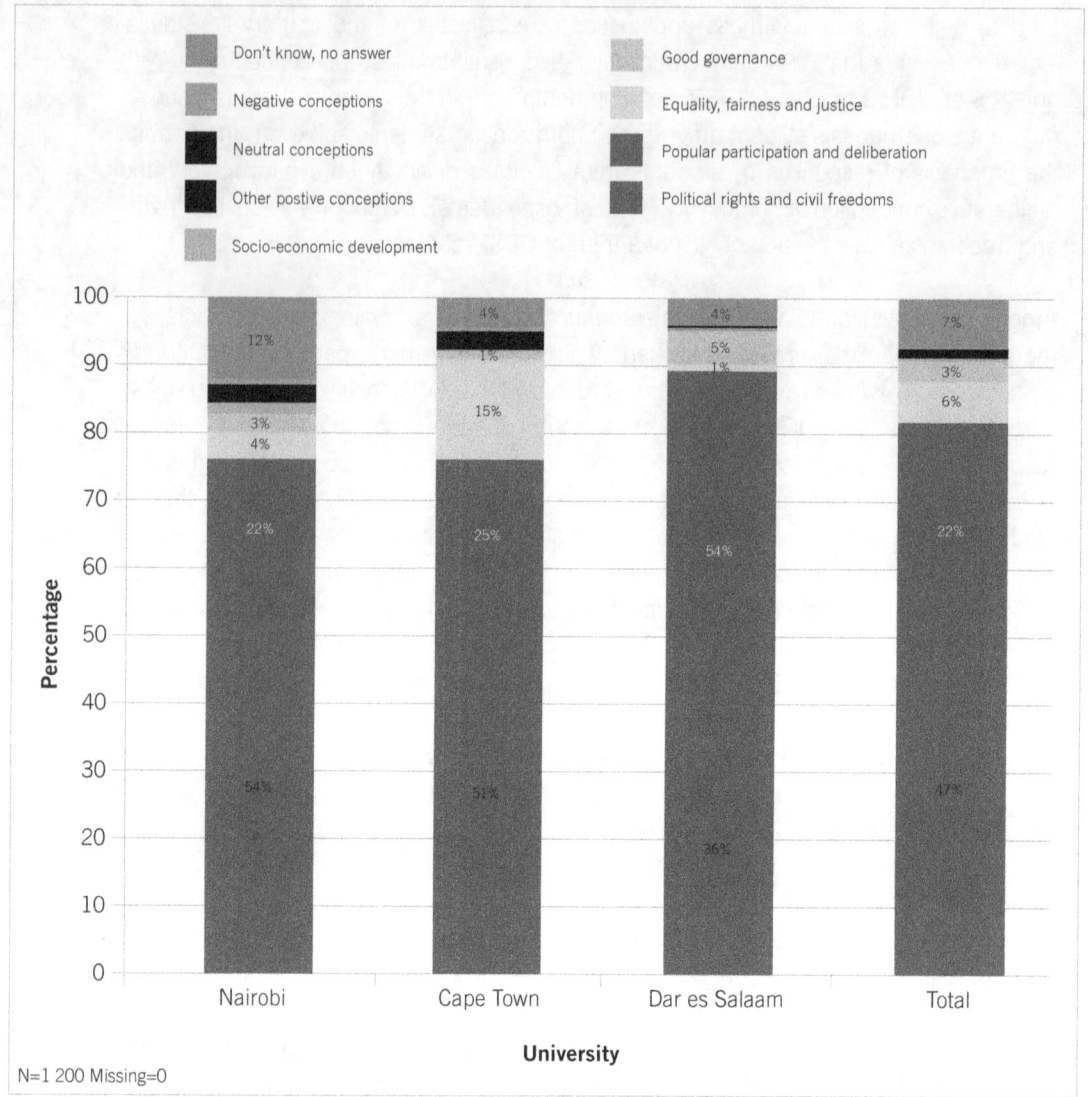

N=1 200 Missing=0

political goods, that is, 'complete freedom for anyone to criticise government' (mean=2.51), 'regular elections' and 'majority rule' (both means=2.45) (compare Table 13).

Table 13 Essential features of democracy

	Mean	N Valid	Std. Deviation
Basic necessities like shelter, food and water for everyone	2.58	1 134	.79
Equality in education	2.56	1 134	.80
Complete freedom to criticise government	2.51	1 128	.75
Majority rule	2.45	1 139	.85
Regular elections	2.45	1 124	.85
Multi-party democracy	2.42	1 127	.92
Jobs for everyone	2.28	1 132	.89
A small income gap between rich and poor	2.19	1 135	1.04

Central tendency values and dispersion of responses to the question: 'In order for a country to be called a "democracy", please tell me which ones of the following features do you think is essential or not important at all?' Responses on Likert scale 0=not at all important; 1=not very important; 2=somewhat important; 3=absolutely important.

Therefore, even though students define democracy in rather liberal and procedural terms when not prompted (i.e. in their own words), it is evident that once they are confronted with a tempting wishlist, the tendency is towards more substantive elements of democracy associated with social equality. Universal access to basic necessities and equality in education, have apparently the greatest appeal. However, overall the least support (and greatest dispersion) can be observed in the response to purely economic goods offered, that is, 'full employment' (mean=2.28) and 'income equality' (mean=2.19). Are these latter choices – while still considered as important for a democracy – perhaps too unrealistic to attain even from a students' perspective?

When considering the student responses by university a number of anomalies emerge (see Table 14). It can be seen that despite the emphasis on democracy as 'equality' observed in the UCT responses (above), UCT students are now the least likely of the three student groups to consider socio-economic equality as 'absolutely essential'. The emphasis is rather on multi-party competition and elections. Conversely, it is the students at the University of Nairobi who emerge as the most supportive of substantial socio-economic outcomes as absolutely essential features of democracy (rather than their poorer counterparts at UDSM). And lastly, Tanzanian students appear now as the champions of democracy as 'majority rule' while without having being prompted in the earlier question, this notion of democracy was largely absent in the UDSM sample.

Table 14 Essential features of democracy by university

	University			Total
	Nairobi	Cape Town	Dar es Salaam	
Majority rule	62%	54%	72%	63%
Complete freedom for everyone to criticize the government	64%	63%	64%	64%
Regular elections	59%	81%	51%	64%
At least two political parties competing with each other	56%	84%	55%	65%
Having necessities like shelter, food and water for everyone	85%	65%	68%	73%
Jobs for everyone	62%	44%	48%	52%
Equality in education	78%	65%	70%	71%
Small income gap between rich and poor	72%	36%	54%	54%

'In order for a country to be called a "democracy", please tell me which ones of the following features do you think is essential or not important at all?'
% 'Absolutely essential'

3.3 Preference for democracy over other regime types

3.3.1 Support for democracy

Students at the Universities of Cape Town, Dar es Salaam and Nairobi do not only understand what democracy is; they also show preference for democracy over non-democratic forms of government. Seven in ten respondents across the three campuses (69%) are supportive of democracy, saying that in their opinion, 'Democracy is preferable to any other kind of government'. This figure is equivalent to that reported by the Africa-wide Afrobarometer surveys (Gyimah-Boadi & Armah Attoh 2009).

Table 15 Preference for democracy by university

	University			Total
	Nairobi	Cape Town	Dar es Salaam	
Democracy is preferable to any other kind of government	266	279	246	791
	70.4%	72.3%	65.3%	69.3%
In some circumstances a non-democratic government can be preferred	85	79	78	242
	22.5%	20.5%	20.7%	21.2%
For someone like me it doesn't matter what kind of government we have	27	28	53	108
	7.1%	7.3%	14.1%	9.5%
Total (N valid)	**378**	**386**	**377**	**1 141**
	100.0%	100.0%	100.0%	100.0%

% and count of 'Which statement is closest to your opinion?'

As Table 15 shows, the cross-country figures mask significant differences between the student bodies of the three universities. Students at the University of Cape Town are marginally more supportive of democracy (72%) than students at the University of Nairobi (70%). At Dar es Salaam University, 65% of students explicitly prefer democracy. However, the lower support for democracy there does not immediately translate into greater preference for non-democratic government; rather the number of students at UDSM who express *indifference* towards the question is almost double than that in Nairobi and in Cape Town. In other questions (below) it will be shown, however, that the students in Dar es Salaam seem to be slightly more inclined towards non-democratic government than their peers in Kenya and South Africa.

The within-country comparison of the student survey results with their peers from the same age cohort who do not have higher education and with the mass public at large shows that in Kenya and Tanzania, the university student preference towards democracy closely resembles that of their (countrywide) age cohort, but is significantly lower than preference for democracy by Kenyans and Tanzanians at large. The UCT students, in contrast, emerge as 'champions of democracy' within their age cohort and, to a lesser extent, in comparison to mass public opinion (compare Figure 11).

3.3.2 Rejection of non-democratic alternatives

The corollary to questions of the extent to which students understand the idea of 'democracy' and its diverse features and express preference for democratic rule is the question how much they also reject authoritarian alternatives to democracy which may present themselves or have been part of the political history of their country or its neighbours. To assess this question, the Student Governance Survey asked students to express their approval/disapproval of three non-democratic regime types: one-party rule; military rule; and presidential strongman rule.

CHAPTER 3 STUDENTS' DEMAND FOR DEMOCRACY AND FREEDOM

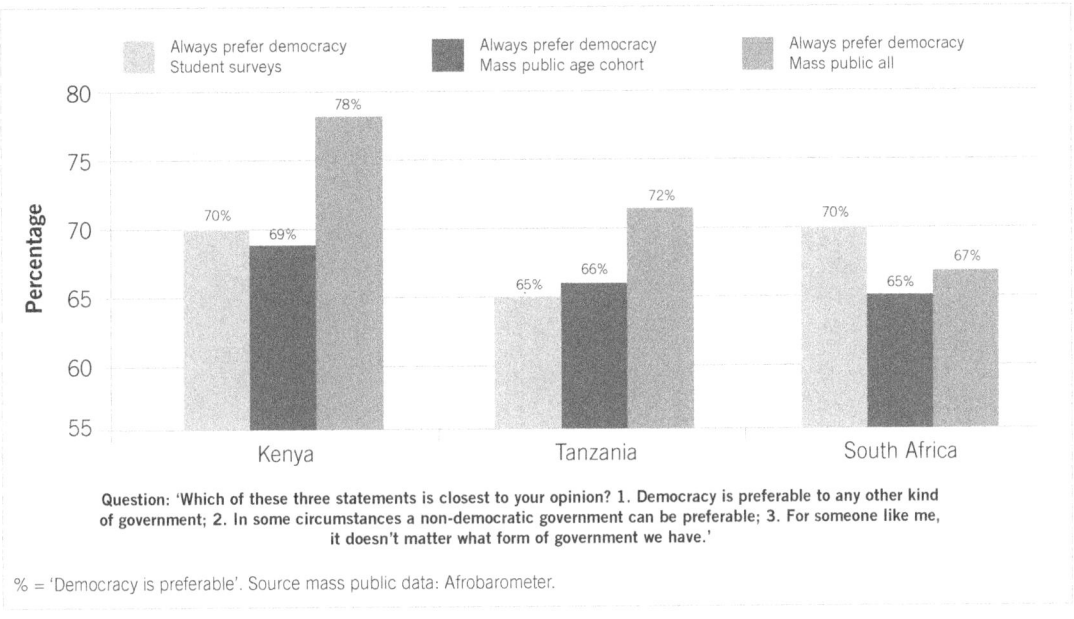

Figure 11 Students' preference for democracy in comparative perspective

Question: 'Which of these three statements is closest to your opinion? 1. Democracy is preferable to any other kind of government; 2. In some circumstances a non-democratic government can be preferable; 3. For someone like me, it doesn't matter what form of government we have.'

% = 'Democracy is preferable'. Source mass public data: Afrobarometer.

Table 16 Rejection of non-democratic alternatives by university

	University			Total
	Nairobi	Cape Town	Dar es Salaam	
Reject one-party rule	80%	84%	81%	82%
Reject military rule	90%	94%	77%	87%
Reject president strongman rule	97%	93%	89%	93%

Question: 'There are many ways to govern a country. Would you approve of the following alternative? (1) If only one party is allowed to stand for an election and hold office; (2) If the army comes in to govern the country; (3) If elections and parliament are abolished so that the president can decide everything'. % 'Strongly disapprove' / 'Disapprove'.
N=1 200 Missing=84

Table 16 shows that overall, presidential strongman rule receives the highest rejection by students (93% disapproval); followed by disapproval of military rule (87%) and one-party rule (82%). Conversely, almost 12% of respondents across the three campuses would 'approve' or even 'strongly approve' of one-party rule.

Variations in student responses between the three campuses and in comparison to the mass sample are shown in Figure 12 to Figure 14. As illustrated in Figure 12, 90% of the UON students reject military rule, which is only marginally lower than Kenyans in general and their age cohort (94% rejection each). In South Africa, military rule is rejected by a far greater majority of UCT students (94% 'disapprove/strongly disapprove') than their age peers without higher education (only 59% reject) and than South Africans in general (68% reject). UDSM students are least disapproving of military rule of the three student bodies; yet still over 77% of Dar es Salaam students reject military rule (against almost 13% of students at UDSM who would approve of a military regime). UDSM students are not only less critical of military rule than their student peers in Nairobi and Cape Town, they are also significantly less critical of military rule than Tanzanians of their age cohort (88% reject)

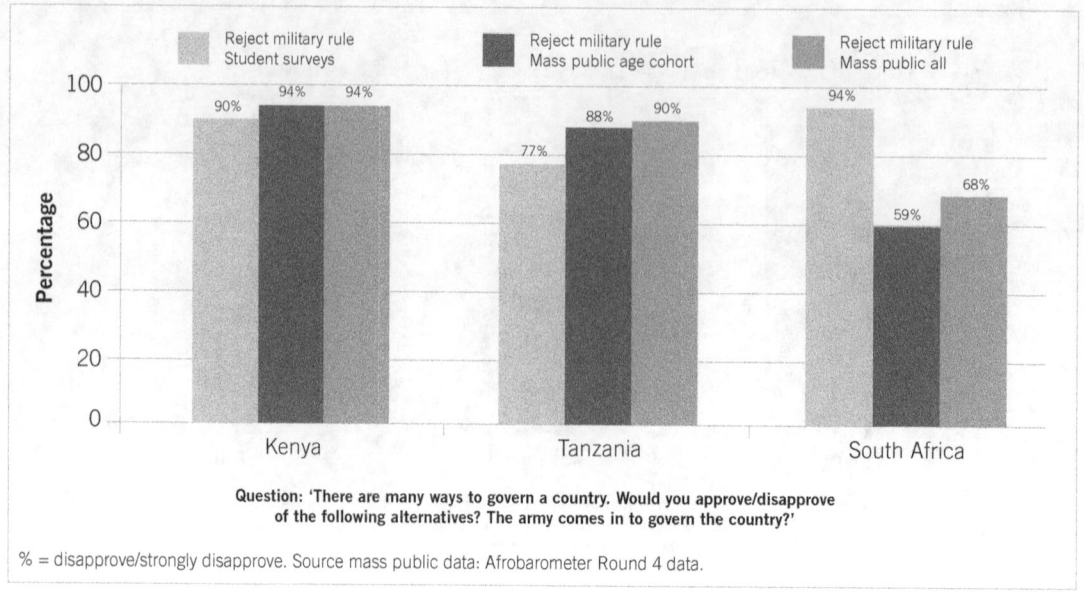

Figure 12 Students' rejection of military rule in comparative perspective

Question: 'There are many ways to govern a country. Would you approve/disapprove of the following alternatives? The army comes in to govern the country?'

% = disapprove/strongly disapprove. Source mass public data: Afrobarometer Round 4 data.

and the Tanzanian public in general, of which 90% reject the army coming in to govern the country.

With respect to one-party rule (Figure 13 below), students appear more critical than their age cohort without university education and mass publics in general. Only in Kenya is the proportion of the public and students who reject one-party rule the same (80% each). In Tanzania and South Africa, however, significantly more students than nationals reject this alternative to multi-party democracy. At UDSM, 81% of students disapprove of one party

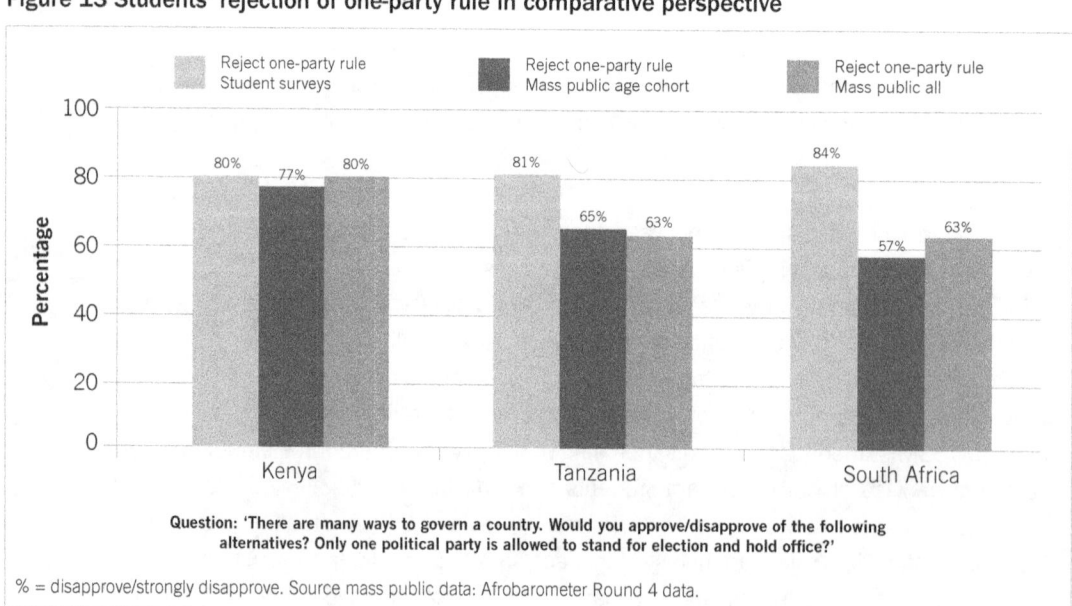

Figure 13 Students' rejection of one-party rule in comparative perspective

Question: 'There are many ways to govern a country. Would you approve/disapprove of the following alternatives? Only one political party is allowed to stand for election and hold office?'

% = disapprove/strongly disapprove. Source mass public data: Afrobarometer Round 4 data.

rule (against only 65% of their age cohort and 63% of the mass public). At UCT 84% of students reject one-party rule (as against only 57% of their age cohort and 63% of the South African public in general).

The relatively low disapproval of one-party rule by the mass publics of Tanzania and South Africa could be seen as a tacit endorsement of the dominant party system by a large section in the respective countries; while the higher disapproval of it by students could be seen conversely as their disapproval of the dominant status of the ruling party. Moreover, UCT students again emerge as considerably more anti-non-democratic rule than their age cohort and the South African public.

Lastly, as far as presidential strongman rule is concerned (Figure 14), the vast majority of students reject this alternative overwhelmingly (UON 97%; UCT 93%; UDSM 89%). The high rejection of strongman rule among the East African students is in keeping with the sentiment of the respective age cohorts. UON students' rejection of presidential rule is, however, significantly higher than that of the Kenyan public (89%); while that of UDSM students is only marginally lower than that of Tanzanians in general (91%). In contrast UCT students again emerge as considerably more democratic than their age peers nationwide (of which only 57% reject strongman rule) and also more democratic than South Africans in general (only 64% reject strongman rule).

Figure 14 Students' rejection of one-man rule in comparative perspective

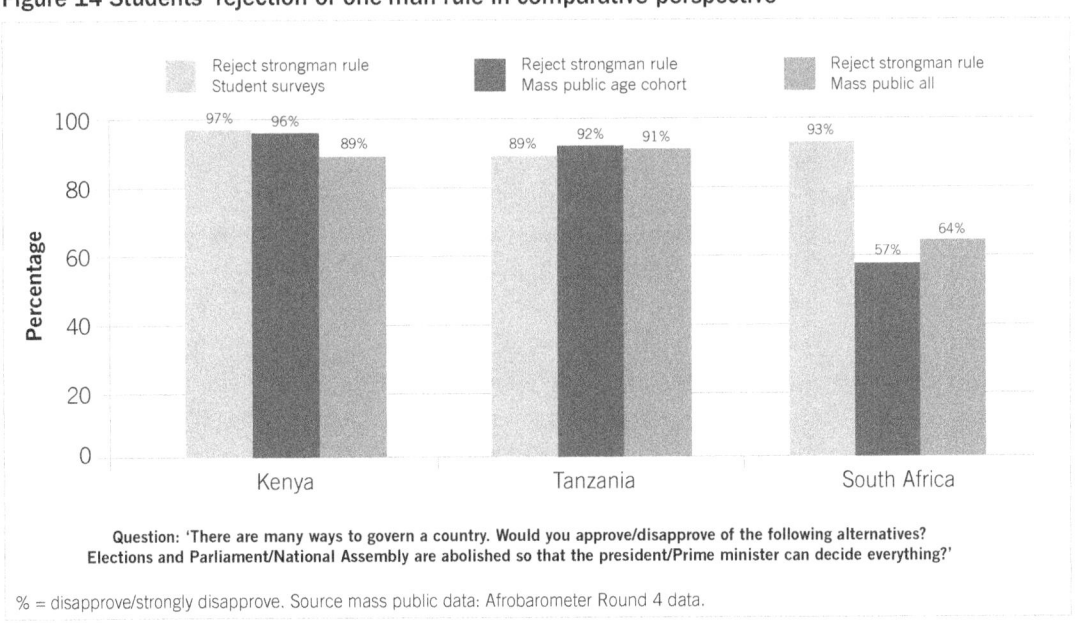

Question: 'There are many ways to govern a country. Would you approve/disapprove of the following alternatives? Elections and Parliament/National Assembly are abolished so that the president/Prime minister can decide everything?'

% = disapprove/strongly disapprove. Source mass public data: Afrobarometer Round 4 data.

The lack of explicit disapproval of authoritarian forms of rule does not automatically translate into expressed support for them. Of the three alternatives, student support is highest for single-party rule; at UON 14% of respondents 'approve/strongly approve' of this form of rule, followed by 12% of UDSM students, and 9% at UCT. The least explicit support across all campuses is for rule by a presidential strong man (<3%). It receives no support from the students in Kenya (<1%), from those in South Africa (<2%), and very little in Tanzania (6%).

Looking at all three non-democratic alternatives combined, the survey finds that there is no significant difference in the attitudes of students in Tanzania and in Kenya compared to the mass public (average rejection at 82% and 89% respectively), but that there is a big difference between UCT students and South Africans in general. UCT students appear distinctly more disapproving of any kind of non-democratic rule than the South African public. While 90% of UCT students reject non-democratic rule, only 58% of their age cohort without university education in the mass public do so, which is even less than the South African mass public in general (of which 65% reject it). It is at once shocking that only just over half of 20–23 year old South Africans without higher education reject non-democratic forms of rule, and encouraging that among UCT students the proportion who disapprove of authoritarian rule is overwhelmingly high (90%).

3.4 Demand for political freedoms

The pursuit of multi-party democracy requires a number of basic political freedoms to operate successfully. Key among them is: freedom of speech, freedom of the press and freedom of association. The Student Governance Surveys investigated student support for these freedoms by asking them to agree/disagree with positive and negative statements that indicate the presence or absence of a particular freedom.

Several observations can be made from the data (see Table 17). It is evident that the majority of the students (in some cases a vast majority) reject or even strongly reject all statements that suggest government should be able to curtail free speech, freedom of association and press freedom. Overall 86% of students reject government interference in press freedom; 73% reject the banning of organisations that go against government's views; and 69% reject governmental limitations on free speech.

However, the corollary positive statements that suggest unfettered political freedoms receive more varied levels of support. Generally speaking, the students more strongly *disagree* with statements that limit political freedoms than they agree with unfettered rights to free speech, free association and press freedom. This suggests a rather nuanced demand for these freedoms; a demand which may actually be compatible with the earlier observations of the students' understandings of democracy, whereby democracy is not simply conceived as a political system of rights and freedoms but one which also involves citizen participation in decision-making (and perhaps other kinds of citizen duties?). This combination actually evokes more republican notions of citizenship which classically involve not only freedoms and rights but also corollary duties and constraints on individual freedoms in the interest of the common good. Table 17 provides a detailed overview of students' demand for freedom by campus and across all campuses.

Table 17 Students' demand for political freedoms

		University			Total / N valid
		Nairobi	Cape Town	Dar es Salaam	
Freedom of speech					
Negative	'Government should not allow the expression of political views that are fundamentally different from the views of the majority'. % disagree / disagree strongly	70%	81%	55%	69% 1 146
Positive	'People should be able to speak their minds about politics free of government influence'. % agree / agree strongly	82%	80%	81%	81% 1 144
Freedom of association					
Negative	'Government should be able to ban any organisation that goes against its views'. % disagree / disagree strongly	78%	84%	57%	73% 1 136
Positive	'People should be able to start and join any organisation they like, whether the government approves it or not'. % agree / agree strongly	34%	70%	43%	49% 1 138
Freedom of press					
Negative	'Government should be able to close newspapers that print stories it does not like' % disagree / disagree strongly	88%	88%	82%	86% 1 141
Positive	'The news media should be free to publish any story that they see fit without fear of being shut down'. % agree / agree strongly	79%	84%	84%	82% 1 140

Question: 'Do you agree or disagree with the following statements?' %=demand for freedom

Table 18 Demand for freedom index by country and university

		Mean	N Valid	Std.Dev.
Kenya	UON students	2.21	375	.4822
	Age cohort	2.14	157	.7759
	Mass public	2.04	1 104	.768
South Africa	UCT students	2.42	374	.4657
	Age cohort	2.07	312	.731
	Mass public	2.17	2 400	.688
Tanzania	UDSM students	2.11	361	.4804
	Age cohort	1.67	162	.786
	Mass public	1.64	1 208	.804

0 = demand for complete unfreedom; 3 = demand for perfect freedom

From Table 17 and Table 18 it can also be seen that overall respondents at the University of Cape Town have consistently the highest demand for all three freedoms. Support for unfettered press freedom is highest (support ranges between 84–88%), followed by demand for freedom of association (70–84%) and free speech (80–81%). On the mean scale of Table 18 where 0 = perfect demand for government restrictions/unfreedom and 3 = perfect demand for freedoms, students at UCT have by far the highest mean score of 2.42. They also demand all political freedoms far more than their 20–23 year age peers who are not in higher education, and more likely than South Africans in general.

Second highest is the demand for political freedom by students of the University of Nairobi. Of them 79–88% demand press freedom and 70–82% demand free speech, but UON students seem to be more sceptical towards unfettered freedom of association (support ranges between 34–78%). On the mean scale Table 18, UON students score a mean value of 2.21 in their demand for political freedoms as against 2.07 of their age cohort and 2.17 of the Kenyan public overall.

Except for a high demand for unrestricted press freedom (82–84%), students from the University of Dar es Salaam have mixed feelings towards unfettered free speech (support range 55–81%) and only about half support unlimited freedom of association (43–57%). On the mean scale, UDSM students score 2.11; their age cohort and Tanzanians in general are, however, far less likely to support unfettered political freedoms (scoring 1.67 and 1.64 respectively on the mean scale). The latter means that only just over half of Tanzanians (51.1%) demand political freedoms above granting government the right to make drastic restrictions (such as closing critical newspapers, banning organisations, and prohibiting the expression of unpopular views). It is also significant that the standard deviation is far wider in the mass samples than the more 'compact' student samples.

3.5 Students as committed democrats?

It has been shown that a vast majority of students at the Universities of Cape Town, Dar es Salaam and Nairobi understand what democracy is, support democracy and reject various alternative, non-democratic forms of government. However, can these students be considered 'committed democrats'? And if so, is political participation a useful determinant that can help explain their commitment?

3.5.1 Commitment to democracy by university

The notion of 'committed democrats' defines those respondents who have consistently displayed high demand for democracy in that they 'always prefer democracy' and 'always reject non-democratic regime alternatives' when offered the choice. These requirements, which are measured by four different indicators in the questionnaire, represent a rather stringent set of requirements. Table 19 indicates that consistent demand for democracy among students of the three surveyed universities is such that only at the University of Cape Town can the majority of the students (54%) be called committed democrats. At the University of Nairobi only 45% of the respondents consistently demand democracy and always reject any kind of authoritarian government, and at the University of Dar es Salaam the corresponding number of students is even lower with only 36% committed democrats.

Table 19 Committed democrats by university

			University			Total
			Nairobi	Cape Town	Dar es Salaam	
Committed democrat?	Yes	Count	181	217	146	543
		%	45%	54%	36%	45%
	No	Count	219	183	254	657
		%	55%	46%	64%	55%
Total		Count	400	400	400	1 200
		% within	100%	100%	100%	100%

N=1 200 Missing=0

The findings of Table 19 thus mirror the earlier findings that UCT students most consistently prefer democracy and reject non-democratic government (followed by UON students), while UDSM students are more often ambiguous or less clearly committal. Putting the student figures into national perspective provides a way of interpreting the data.

3.5.2 Commitment to democracy in national comparative perspective

Once students' commitment to democracy is looked at within the context of the mass public opinion surveys of their countries, it emerges that the UCT students' views are more likely an 'outlier' as their results are widely divergent from their respective comparative samples (but more comparative work would be needed to pronounce strongly on that). As Figure 15 indicates, overall, the East African students emerge as considerably less committed to democracy than their respective mass publics, while their respective age cohorts without higher education in the mass public straddle the two extremes. Thus, whereas only 45% of UON students qualify as committed democrats, it is 55% in the same Kenyan age cohort and 63% of Kenyans in general who would qualify. Similarly in Tanzania, only 36% of UDSM students can be defined as committed democrats, while the corresponding figure is 43% among their age reference group and 46% among Tanzanians in general. On the basis of these comparisons it could be argued that if anything, high levels of education and youthfulness seems to contribute to *less* commitment to democracy.

Figure 15 Committed democrats

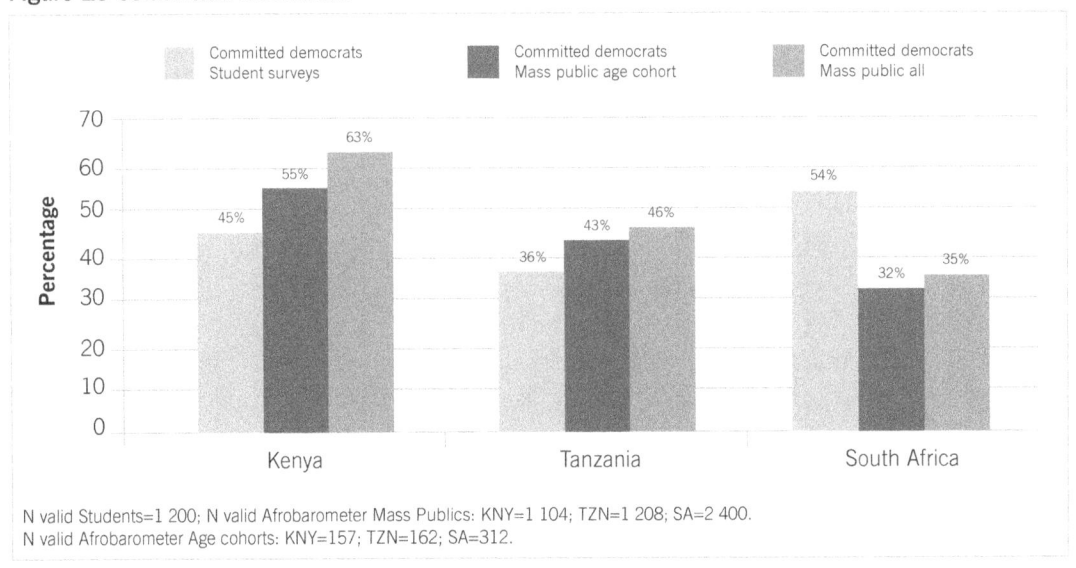

N valid Students=1 200; N valid Afrobarometer Mass Publics: KNY=1 104; TZN=1 208; SA=2 400.
N valid Afrobarometer Age cohorts: KNY=157; TZN=162; SA=312.

The UCT students turn out to be pro-democratic 'outliers' not only in the inter-university but also in the intra-country comparison. While 54% of UCT students are committed democrats, only 35% of South Africans in general can be defined as such, and even less of the youthful South African age cohort without higher education, where only 32% are consistently committed to democracy. The low figures among South African youth (other than UCT students) derive from the combination of a much lower rejection of non-democratic alternatives, and lower expressed preference for democracy. Thus, less than 60% of the South African 20–22 age cohort without higher education reject single party rule (57%), military rule (59%), or presidential dictatorship (57%) while the comparative figures among UCT students range between 84% to 94%. Additionally, there is also a higher preference for democracy per se among UCT students (UCT students: 72%; national age cohort without higher education 65%; SA mass sample 67%) (compare Figure 11 to Figure 14).

3.5.3 Political participation and commitment to democracy

Is political participation among the determinants what makes a committed democrat? In order to test this, we considered two related hypotheses. Firstly we tested whether formal student leaders were significantly more (or less) committed to democracy than other students.

Table 20 Student leaders as committed democrats?

University			Student leader		Total
			No	Yes	
Nairobi	Committed democrat	Yes	45%	42%	45%
		No	55%	58%	55%
Cape Town	Committed democrat	Yes	54%	57%	54%
		No	46%	43%	46%
Dar es Salaam	Committed democrat	Yes	36%	37%	36%
		No	64%	63%	64%

N=1 200 Missing=0

Table 20 shows that there is a fairly even distribution of commitment to democracy between student leaders and students not in leadership across all categories within countries. It is noteworthy that student leaders at the University of Cape Town emerge as the most committed to democracy of all the student groups, while students not in leadership at the University of Dar es Salaam are least likely committed democrats. Thus, overall, student leaders at UDSM and UCT, but not those at UON, emerge as slightly more committed to democracy than the students whom they represent on their respective campuses. However, the correlation shows that the relationship between formal involvement in student leadership and commitment to democracy is *overall not statistically significant*.

A second simple bivariate test related to political participation was performed to see whether student activists, and particularly students who had attended one or more demonstration or protest marches in the past year, were significantly more (or less) committed to democracy than students who had stayed away from political activism.

Table 21 Student activists as committed democrats?

University			Student activist		Total
			No	Yes	
Nairobi	Committed democrat	Yes	45%	52%	47%
		No	55%	48%	53%
Cape Town	Committed democrat	Yes	55%	58%	55%
		No	45%	42%	45%
Dar es Salaam	Committed democrat	Yes	36%	39%	37%
		No	64%	61%	63%

Question: 'Have you been involved in any of the following activities in the past year?'
Choice D: 'Attended a demonstration or protest march.'
Yes='Yes, I was involved'; 'Often' / 'Several times' / 'Once or twice'. No='No'
N=1 200 Missing=37

Table 21 shows that there is some noteworthy variation of commitment to democracy between student activists and students not involved in protest activity. In all three universities, student activists are marginally more likely to be committed democrats. The difference is greatest among students in Nairobi, where 52% of student activists are committed democrats as against 45% of non-activists. Cape Town student activists also emerge as being most likely committed to democracy like the formal student leaders; and students of the University of Dar es Salaam not involved in political protests and demonstrations are the least likely committed democrats. However, the correlation shows that the relationship between involvement in protests and commitment to democracy is overall not statistically significant and no related variables have been controlled for.

3.5.4 Explaining commitment to democracy

Table 22 provides the results of an attempt to explain different levels of commitment to democracy among the students. A number of models were tested including different independent variables. The model displayed in Table 22 includes social background and academic variables; variables relating to students' demand for democracy and perception of supply of democracy; cognitive engagement and political participation variables; as well as other variables (as noted beneath the table). The dependent variable is in all cases a five point index (0–4) measuring students' expressed commitment to democracy (measured as 'prefers democracy' and 'rejects military rule', 'rejects one-party rule', 'rejects presidential dictatorship', as above).[16]

Cognitive awareness variables are the most promising predictors of commitment to democracy. Particularly, political awareness of institutions and incumbents positively contributes to commitment to democracy in both the UON and UCT cases (and when considering all students). It is also interesting to note that use of news media contributes

---

16 Factor analysis extracted a single unrotated factor (Eigen value 1.989) that explains 49.7% of total variance of the four items. Index reliability (Cronbach's Alpha = 0.567) (N=1 411). Factor analysis and reliability analysis were also performed for all other indices that were constructed (indices of independent variables).

negatively (albeit very little) to commitment to democracy at UON and lesser at UDSM. This contradicts findings from mass public data (e.g. Mattes & Mughogho 2010). Of the political participation and attitudes to civil society variables, voting in previous elections (national elections in Kenya, and student elections at UCT) has small positive effects on commitment to democracy. Statistically significant but very small effects are also found among social background variables (male and urban), perceptions of trust (negative effect) and trust in state institutions (negative effect) in some samples. Overall, Table 22 shows very little commonality in what may explain commitment to democracy in the three student bodies apart from the reported effects of political awareness. The explanatory power of the model overall is weak in all three cases.

The most important interesting finding from Table 22 is perhaps what does *not* emerge as significant. As has been noted above, involvement in formal student leadership (measured categorically yes/no) is not a statistically significant predictor for commitment to democracy in any of the three universities. Neither do any of the more sophisticated indices of student political participation emerge as a significant predictor of commitment to democracy (i.e. involvement in formal student leadership index; involvement in activist student politics index). Moreover, the type of funding for university studies that could serve as a potential class proxy (especially in the UCT case, see chapter 2), emerged as not significant in all cases. Neither did faculty of study (albeit only measured in terms of the three different faculty clusters noted in chapter 2) emerge as a significant predictor of democratic commitment.

3.6 Summary and conclusion

This chapter has considered students' demand for democracy and freedom. It has shown that students are well acquainted with democracy as a political system involving popular participation in decision-making, multi-party elections, and a necessary set of political rights and freedoms. Over two-thirds of students prefer democracy to any other regime type and typically over 80% reject any or all offered non-democratic regime alternatives. At the same time demand for freedoms important in a democracy (like press freedom, free speech and freedom of association) is also high, albeit with some reservations.

Using the notion of 'committed democrat' as a touchstone, it emerges that only a minority of UON and UDSM students can be described as committed democrats. Moreover, they emerge as *less* committed to democracy than their national age cohort without higher education and less committed than Kenyans and Tanzanians in general, respectively. Indeed, of all the samples, the Kenyan public appears as 'champions of democracy', that is, the most committed to democracy (as almost two-thirds qualify as 'committed democrats'). While UCT students are not as committed to democracy as the Kenyan public, they are the most committed student group in the inter-university comparison, and in the intra-South African comparison, they are by far more committed to democracy than their age reference group. With regard to higher education's contribution to commitment to democracy per se, the findings of the Student Governance Surveys therefore paint a mixed picture that partially confirms the findings of Mattes and Mughogho (2010). Lastly,

Table 22 Explaining student commitment to democracy

		Background		Political participation & associational membership			Cognitive awareness				Rule of law	Trust	Country sig. (South Africa)	Total adj. R2
		Male	Urban	Voted student election	Voted national election	Off-campus religious membership	Trust state institutions	News media use	Political awareness (NL I&I)	Political awareness (SL I&I)	Perception of corruption (NL)	Trust state institutions		
All three universities	B (Beta)	-.095* (-.066)	.109* (.072)	.101* (.070)	n/s	n/s	.074* (.091)	-.122*** (-.134)	.420*** (.121)	.257* (.089)	n/s	n/s	.182** (.126)	.091
University of Nairobi	B (Beta)	n/s	.167* (.129)	n/s	.214* (.136)	n/s	n/s	-.213*** (-.255)	.508* (.143)	.371* (.149)	-.128* (-.146)	-.107* (-.142)	n/s	.098
University of Cape Town	B (Beta)	n/s	n/s	.214*** (.155)	n/s	.071* (.104)	n/s	n/s	.535*** (.176)	n/s	-.103* (-.121)	n/s	n/a	.132
University Dar es Salaam	B (Beta)	n/s	n/s	n/s	n/s	n/s	.147* (.159)	-.174* (.132)	n/s	n/s	n/s	n/s	n/a	.046

ALL: B=3.027; Std. Error= .232; t=13.026 N=1 411
UON: B=3.889; Std. Error= .391; t=9.935. N=405
UCT: B=2.395; Std. Error= .332; t=7.216. N=606
UDSM: B=2.992; Std. Error= .588; t=5.367. N=400

Dependent variable: Support for Democracy Index; Independent variables (predictors) Model 1:
a. Social Background & Academic Variables: Private main source of financial support; Government main source of financial support; Gender (male); Urban; Faculty Cluster (HUM); Faculty Cluster (SET);
b. Demand for Democracy Variables: Demand for Rights (SL & NL);
c. Supply of Democracy & Rule of Law Variables: Evaluation of representation at national level; Evaluation of NL incumbent performance; Perception of corruption NL index; Perception of leadership accountability index;
d. Cognitive Awareness Variables: News media use index; Discuss politics; Interest in public affairs; SL political awareness (incumbents & institutions) index; NL political awareness (incumbents & institutions) index;
e. Participation/Attitudes to Civil Society Variables: Participation in formal student leadership (SLweighted_r); Involved in student politics index; Formal student leader dummy; Involved in off-campus religious group; Involved in off-campus secular association; Voted SL; Voted NL;
f. Other Variables: Trust students; Trust SL Index; Trust other citizens; Trust state/government institutions index; Macro-economic evaluation index;

a simple test as to whether student political participation (in the form of formal student leadership on-campus or off-campus activism) helps in explaining students' commitment to democracy has so far not yielded statistically significant results. Among all the variables tested, only cognitive awareness (interest in public affairs, awareness of political incumbents and institutions at national and/or student/university level) have a markedly positive effect on commitment to democracy, while news media use has a *negative* effect (in contradistinction to Mattes and Mughogho's findings). The attempt of explaining commitment (or rather support) for democracy is pursued further in the following chapters.

Overall this chapter on students' demand of democracy does not present a very rosy picture. In the Kenyan and Tanzanian cases, not even half of the upcoming, young and highly educated citizens represented by the students at UON and UDSM are consistently committed to democracy; and while just over half of UCT students qualify as 'committed democrats' they, in turn, appear as pro-democratic 'outliers' in the midst of *a less educated peer group* (and mass public) that is considerably less committed to democracy.

Chapter 4
Students' Perception of the Supply of Democracy and Democratic Consolidation

4.1 Introduction

While students' attitudes towards democracy in general may be ambiguous and somewhat difficult to interpret, their views of the current political regime are more likely deeply grounded in their personal experiences and perceptions of politics in their country. How do students view the present political systems of Kenya, South Africa and Tanzania? Does the way government works in these countries actually satisfy students' political demands?

In chapter two it was noted that all three political systems are variably considered as 'flawed democracies' or even 'hybrid democracies' in international comparison. All three countries have experience of a single dominant party system; all students have experienced multi-party elections in their lifetime (and many have participated therein). Nonetheless, the broader political context within which the three student groups grew up is rather different.

- The UON students lived the majority of their lives under the (semi-authoritarian) government of Daniel Arap Moi; they were about eight years old when Moi introduced multi-party elections and 18 years old when Moi eventually left office and KANU lost the 2002 election. By the time of the 2007/2008 post-election violence, they were in their early twenties, and, as will be seen, their responses have been shaped profoundly by this dramatic political crisis and its aftermath.
- Most UDSM students, in contrast, have never lived through significant political turmoil (unless they hail from Zanzibar) and have never experienced a change of ruling party. Most of them were born when Julius Nyerere was still president of Tanzania; they were teenagers when multi-partyism was reintroduced and 22 years old when the current president took office.
- Most of the UCT students are little older than the 1990 cohort of 'Mandela's children'; most of them were born in the late 1980s. They were about four years old when 'apartheid' ended in 1990, about eight years old in 1994 and they have lived for most of their schooling years under ANC rule. Being at UCT, most of them are likely to have lived very privileged lives and attended the best (and racially integrated) schools of the country.

What are the perspectives of these highly educated young African students on the politics of their young democracies? Do they concur with international observers about the extent to which their country is a democracy? Are they the 'critical citizens' who evaluate the existing supply of key democratic features such as free and fair elections with a certain suspicion? And how do the views of students from different universities and countries compare with each other and with the views of their respective mass publics and those of their less educated peer group in their home countries?

This chapter first investigates students' perception of freeness and fairness of elections; their opinion as to the extent to which their country is a democracy; students' satisfaction with current regime performance, and the extent to which multi-party democracy has delivered more political freedoms. The findings of the chapter add a student perspective on the extent to which the three countries can be considered democracies. It concludes by analysing students' views in terms of the notion of 'transformative democrat'. Transformative democrats are defined as those students who always prefer democracy, are critical of the current extent of democracy in their country and impatient for regime change in that they are ready to try something else.

The study shows that almost two-thirds of UON students would readily support democratic transformation in their country; a figure which can be understood when looking at the extent of disequilibrium between the Kenya's students' demand for democracy and their perception of its supply. At UDSM, just under half and at UCT about 40% of students would also endorse trying out something else within a context of high demand for democracy and a critical evaluation of current regime performance. Furthermore, the chapter notes continued disparity between the East Africans and the South Africans. UCT students are generally more satisfied with the way different aspects of democracy work in their country than students on the other two campuses. Thus, despite high demand for democracy, a large proportion of UCT students do not see the need for any urgent and drastic change in the South African political system.

4.2 Perception of the current regime

As a way of evaluating the supply of democracy of the current regime, the Student Governance Survey asked students to consider the following questions: *How would you rate the freeness and fairness of the last national general election?*; *How much of a democracy is [your country] today?*; and *Overall, how satisfied are you with the way democracy works in [your country]?* While the first question refers to a key feature of modern representative (or elite-competitive) multi-party democracy, the latter two are more general. In combination, students' responses to these questions reveal a young highly educated citizenry that is extremely critical of current regime performance and generally less convinced of its democratic nature than their compatriots.

CHAPTER 4 STUDENTS' PERCEPTION OF THE SUPPLY OF DEMOCRACY AND DEMOCRATIC CONSOLIDATION

4.2.1 Freeness and fairness of elections

Given the centrality of the electoral process in the operation of modern democracies, perceptions of the freeness and fairness of the elections are an important way to gauge the popular legitimacy that an electoral regime enjoys. In the Student Governance Survey, students were asked to rate the freeness and fairness of the last national general election. The question was asked irrespective of whether a student had actually voted in the last election or not.

The survey finds that overall only 41% of the students (N valid=1 166) consider the previous national election 'completely free and fair' or 'free and fair, but with minor problems'. The majority of students rated the previous elections as flawed in serious ways (compare Table 23).

Table 23 Free and fair elections?

	University			Total
	Nairobi	Cape Town	Dar es Salaam	
Completely free and fair	2%	27%	8%	12%
Free and fair but with minor problems	5%	47%	36%	29%
Free and fair with major problems	18%	11%	22%	17%
Not free and fair	70%	4%	28%	34%
Don't know	4%	11%	7%	7%

Question: 'How would you rate the freeness and fairness of the last national general election?'
N=1 200 Missing=35

Table 23 illustrates why such a large proportion of students rate the freeness and fairness of their last national election so badly. The effect is predominantly due to the responses of the Kenyan students, who overwhelmingly (88%) reject the last general election (November 2007), as riddled with 'major problems'/'not free and fair'. The 2007 presidential election in Kenya is widely considered as flawed. By contrast, the last South African general election (parliamentary election, April 2009) is considered by almost three quarters of UCT students as free and fair (either 'completely free and fair' or 'free and fair, but with minor problems'). Lastly, UDSM students are generally critical in their rating of the last general election in Tanzania: Those who consider the 2005 elections as substantially free and fair are slightly fewer than those who consider it flawed. Figure 16 illustrates these significant differences in students' perception of the supply of electoral democracy through free and fair national elections.

4.2.2 Extent of democracy

Different evaluations of the supply of democracy can also be observed when asking students to rate the extent to which their country is a democracy. The majority of students across all the campuses are reluctant to afford their country the label of being a 'full democracy' or a 'democracy with minor problems'. Indeed, on and across all campuses, the majority of students view their respective country as either a 'democracy with major problems' or even 'not a democracy' at all (see Table 24).

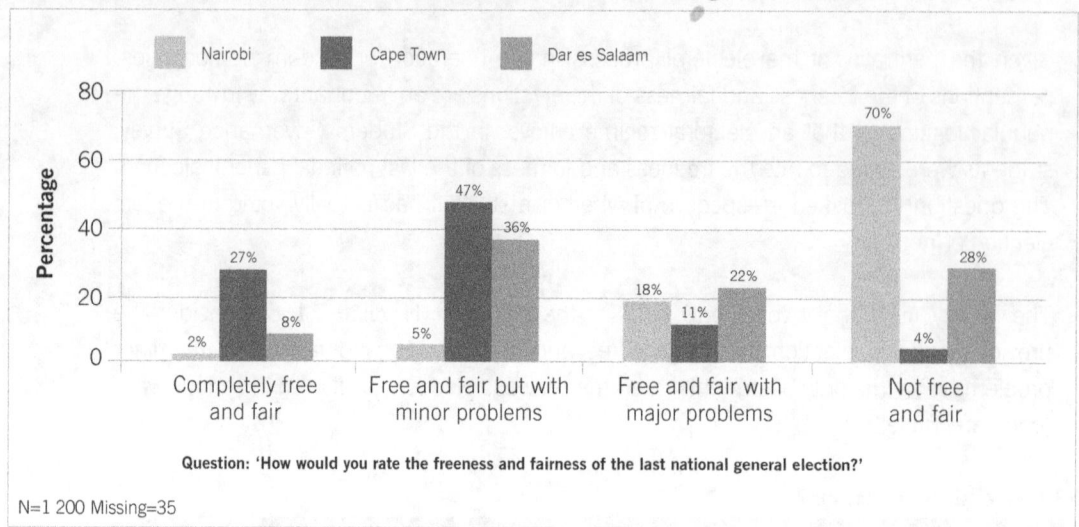

Figure 16 Students' rating of the freeness and fairness of the last general election

Question: 'How would you rate the freeness and fairness of the last national general election?'
N=1 200 Missing=35

Table 24 Students' rating of the extent of democracy in their country

	University			Total
	Nairobi	Cape Town	Dar es Salaam	
A full democracy	2%	6%	3%	4%
A democracy but with minor problems	13%	42%	31%	29%
A democracy with major problems	66%	49%	51%	55%
Not a democracy	20%	3%	15%	13%

Question: 'In your opinion, how much of a democracy is [your country] today?'
N=1 200 Missing=72

As seen in the previous question, students of the University of Nairobi are again the most critical of the democratic nature of governance in their country, followed by students at the University of Dar es Salaam. Two-thirds of student responses from Nairobi view Kenya as a 'democracy with major problems' and another 20% even see it as 'not a democracy' at all. At UDSM, two-thirds of responses see Tanzania either as a 'democracy with major problems' or 'not a democracy', while one-third consider it as a democracy without or with minor problems. More positive in their evaluation are the South Africans. Almost half of the students at the University of Cape Town consider South Africa as either a 'democracy with minor problems' or even a 'full democracy' (48%) (as per Table 24).

In comparative perspective, the Student Governance Surveys show that students are considerably *more critical* of the extent of democracy in their country than their respective age cohort in the mass sample and their fellow citizens in general (see Figure 17).

According to the mass public survey of 2008, 74% of Tanzanians say their country is a full or almost full democracy, against only 65% of young (22–26 year old) Tanzanians and 34% of the surveyed UDSM students. The extent of democracy is even more critically viewed by UON students than their compatriots: Whereas 43% of Kenyans consider their country a 'democracy with minor problems' or even a 'full democracy' (in 2008!), only

Figure 17 Students' rating of the extent of democracy in comparative perspective

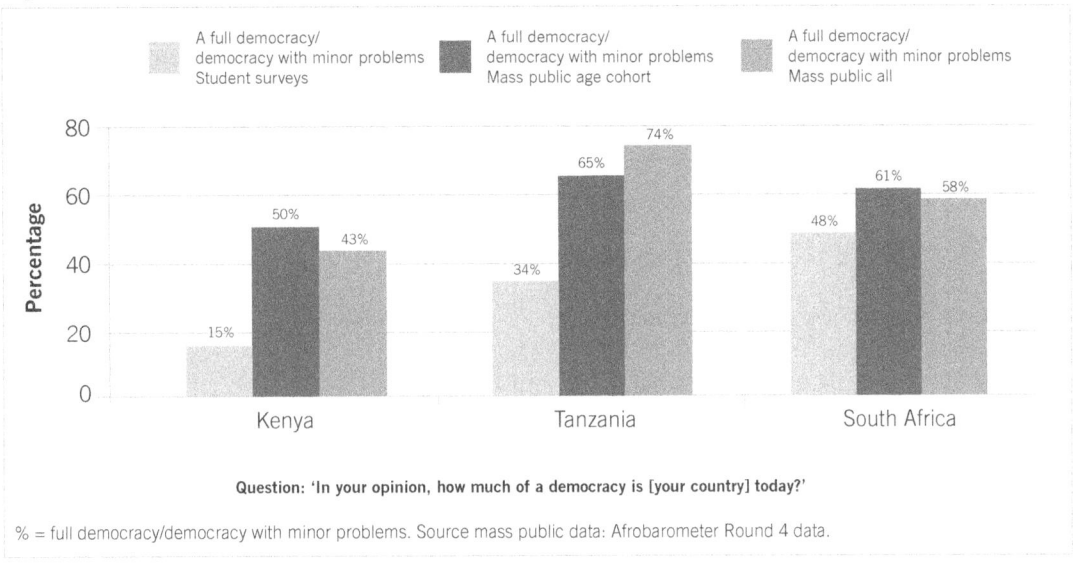

Question: 'In your opinion, how much of a democracy is [your country] today?'

% = full democracy/democracy with minor problems. Source mass public data: Afrobarometer Round 4 data.

15% of UON students do so a year later. Lastly, in South Africa, perceptions of the extent to which South Africa is a democracy are within a narrower range (13 percentage points as against over 30 percentage points in KNY/TZN). UCT students are more in tune with the national perception whereby almost half the students (48%) consider South Africa a full or almost full democracy, along with 61% of their less educated age group and 58% of South Africans in general.

4.2.3 Satisfaction with regime performance

Regardless of the perception of the extent of democracy supplied at national level, students were also asked to rate their satisfaction with the way democracy actually works in their country. The response choices in the questionnaire ranged from being 'very satisfied' with the way democracy works to 'not at all satisfied' and the dismissing statement that my country is 'not a democracy'.

Table 25 indicates that merely a third of the students in the survey are 'very or fairly satisfied' with the way democracy works in their country. Two-thirds are indeed 'not very satisfied', 'not at all satisfied', or even say that their country is 'not a democracy'.

Table 25 Students' satisfaction with democracy in their country

	University			Total
	Nairobi	Cape Town	Dar es Salaam	
Very satisfied	1%	5%	1%	2%
Fairly satisfied	12%	52%	29%	31%
Not very satisfied	36%	36%	44%	39%
Not at all satisfied/ Not a democracy	51%	8%	26%	28%

Question: 'Overall, how satisfied are you with the way democracy works in [country]? Are you...'
N=1 200 Missing=66

In keeping with the earlier observations, the Kenyan students are the least satisfied with democratic performance in their country. The majority of respondents from UON (51%) say that they are 'not at all satisfied' with the way democracy works in Kenya or even that their country is 'not a democracy'. Another 36% of Kenyan students say that they are 'not very satisfied'; leaving only 13% to express some level of satisfaction ('very satisfied'/'fairly satisfied') with current regime performance. In that UON students are also considerably less satisfied and more critical than their compatriots in general, of which 42% are *fairly or very satisfied* with democracy in Kenya (Figure 18).

Figure 18 Students' satisfaction with democracy in comparative perspective

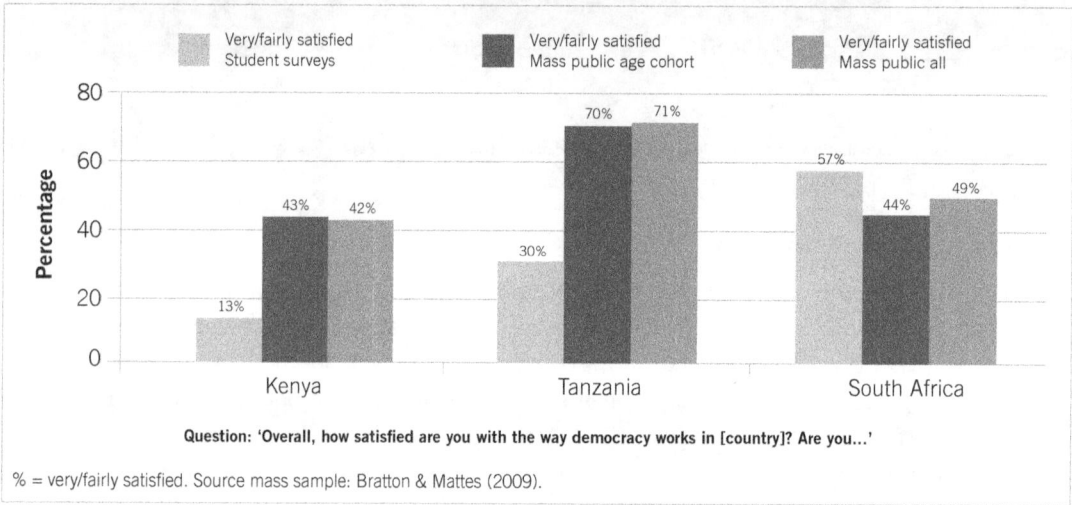

Question: 'Overall, how satisfied are you with the way democracy works in [country]? Are you...'

% = very/fairly satisfied. Source mass sample: Bratton & Mattes (2009).

At the University of Dar es Salaam, just under a third of the students express satisfaction with the way democracy works in Tanzania; while more than two-thirds must be considered as dissatisfied, saying that they are 'not very satisfied' or 'not at all satisfied' with democracy's performance. This is in stark contrast to the mass public in general and their age cohort. The Afrobarometer finds that 71% of Tanzanians are *fairly or very satisfied* with democracy in Tanzania (Figure 18).

The greatest satisfaction with the way democracy works in their country is expressed by the UCT students. Unlike the students on the other campuses, the average UCT student is 'fairly satisfied' by the way democracy works in the country. Only 8% of the South African students are 'not at all satisfied' or say the country is 'not a democracy' (as against 51% in Kenya and 26% in Tanzania). In their satisfaction with democracy in South Africa, UCT students are again closer to the findings from the mass survey of the Afrobarometer than the UON/UDSM students. 49% of South Africans and 44% of the 20–23 age cohort without higher education express good satisfaction with democracy in their country (as against 57% at UCT). These findings of the Student Governance Survey are illustrated in Figure 18.

4.3 Has multi-party democracy supplied more political freedoms?

Provided that democracy is conceived by a large group of students not only in terms of political procedures (e.g. elections) but also in terms of political rights and freedoms, a further way to measure students' perception of the supply of democracy in their country is to ask how students perceive the extent to which the current regime provides them with certain freedoms. In particular, the survey asks whether students feel 'completely free', 'somewhat free', 'not very free' or 'not at all free' to exercise freedom of speech, freedom of association, and free choice in voting.

The survey finds that students consider themselves most free to join whatever political association they want, followed by their perception of freedom to vote for whoever they choose, and least free to say whatever they want. Overall, an overwhelming majority of students across all the three universities feel that they are 'somewhat free'/'completely free' to associate with any political organisation or vote for whoever they choose, and the majority of students at UON and UCT (and close to a majority at UDSM) also feel that they have considerable freedom of speech (see Table 26).

Table 26 Students' perception of the supply of political freedoms

	University			Total
	Nairobi	Cape Town	Dar es Salaam	
Freedom of speech 'say what you want'	53%	82%	48%	61%
Freedom of association 'to join any political organisation you want'	81%	87%	86%	85%
Freedom of voting 'to choose who to vote for without feeling pressured'	76%	89%	78%	81%

% 'Somewhat free' / 'Completely free'
N valid Freedom of Speech: Total 1 158; UON 386; UCT 388; UDSM 384. Freedom of Association: Total 1 154; UON 385; UCT 386; UDSM 383. Freedom of Voting: Total 1 153; UON 383; UCT 385; UDSM 385.

Moreover, when considering the supply of political freedoms perceived by the different student populations it emerges that students at the University of Cape Town consistently consider themselves freer than their counterparts in Nairobi and Dar es Salaam.

With regard to freedom of speech, students across all campuses are most sceptical of the extent of their freedom to say what they want. Only about half of the students on the Nairobi campus (53%) and on the Dar es Salaam campus (48%) consider themselves 'somewhat'/'completely free' to speak their political views. In contrast, at the University of Cape Town, students' perception of freedom of speech is very high, with over 80% feeling 'completely free' or at least 'somewhat free'. Comparing the student responses with Afrobarometer data shows that the students of UDSM and UON are significantly more sceptical of their freedom of speech than their compatriots in general, while UCT students feel about as free to speak their minds as South Africans in general (Figure 19).

Freedom of association is perceived to be more widely enjoyed than other freedoms. At all the three universities, a very clear majority of students (over 80%) feel free to join any political organisation of their choice. Those who feel 'not very free' or 'not at all free 'are in

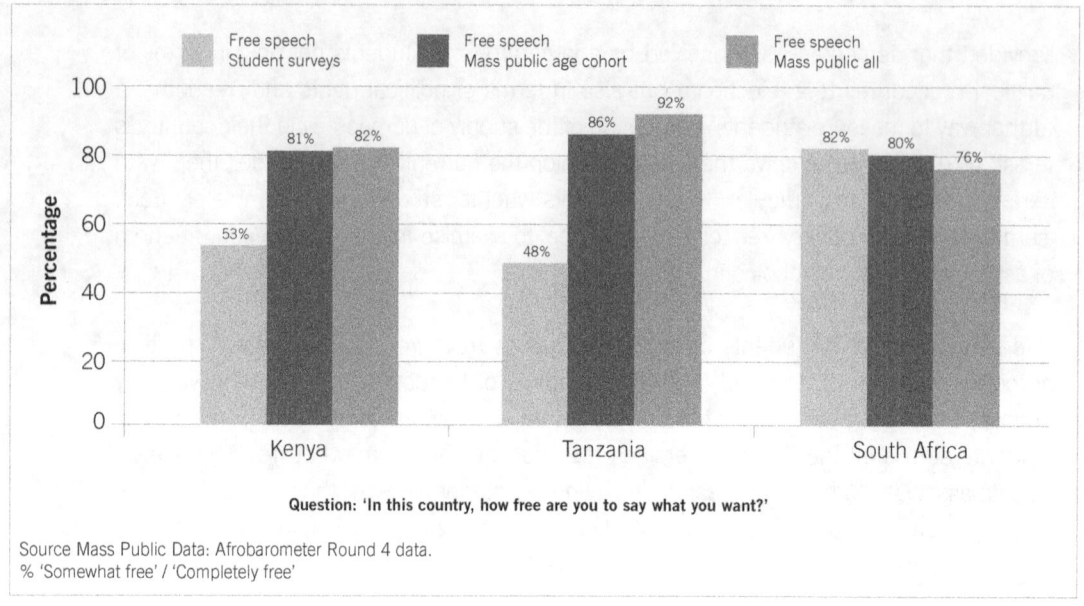

Figure 19 Students' perception of free speech in comparative perspective

Question: 'In this country, how free are you to say what you want?'
Source Mass Public Data: Afrobarometer Round 4 data.
% 'Somewhat free' / 'Completely free'

all cases less than a fifth (19% at UON; 14% at UDSM; 13% UCT). In comparison to the mass publics, students at UON and UDSM still appear slightly more critical of the extent of their freedom of association, while UCT students again perceive themselves freer to join political organisations of their choice than South Africans in general or their age cohort without higher education (see Figure 20).

Lastly, there is significant variation in students' perception of voting freedom across the three countries. On the one hand, a very clear majority of students from all the three universities feel 'somewhat free' or 'completely free' to choose who to vote for without feeling pressured. On the other hand, it also clearly emerges that there is a considerable group of Kenyan students who feel their freedom is not sufficiently guaranteed (24%) and Tanzanian students (21%) who feel 'not at all free' or 'not very free' to make their elective choice unpressured. Within the national landscape, it again emerges that the students at the two East African universities are more critical of the extent of their freedom of voting than Kenyans and Tanzanians in general and their age cohorts, and that UCT students' perception of the freeness of their vote exceeds that of the South African population at large and their age cohort within that (compare Figure 21).

A factor analysis of the student responses indicates that the three freedoms indeed measure the same underlying notion of 'political freedom'. An index with a mean scale from 0 to 3 (whereby 0 refers to complete unfreedom and 3 to perfect freedom) shows that overall UCT students score the highest on the index of perceptions of political freedoms, followed at a distance by Tanzanian students. The recent experience of political turmoil in Kenya in the wake of the flawed presidential election of 2007 has clearly left scars on UON students' perception of the extent of political freedom afforded to them in their country (see Table 27).

CHAPTER 4 STUDENTS' PERCEPTION OF THE SUPPLY OF DEMOCRACY AND DEMOCRATIC CONSOLIDATION

Figure 20 Students' perception of freedom of association in comparative perspective

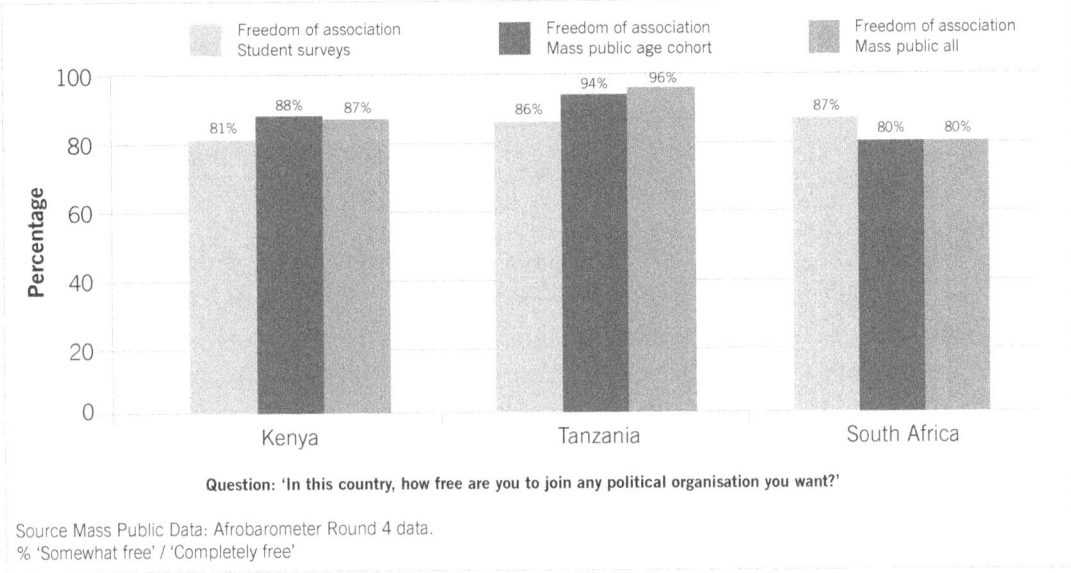

Question: 'In this country, how free are you to join any political organisation you want?'

Source Mass Public Data: Afrobarometer Round 4 data.
% 'Somewhat free' / 'Completely free'

Figure 21 Students' perception of voting freedom in comparative perspective

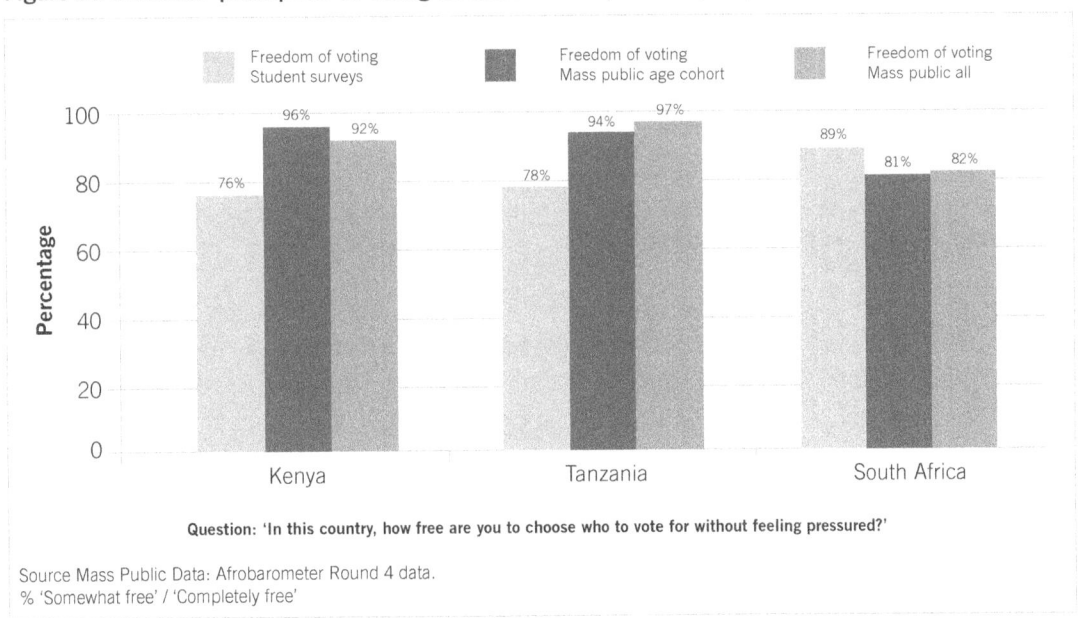

Question: 'In this country, how free are you to choose who to vote for without feeling pressured?'

Source Mass Public Data: Afrobarometer Round 4 data.
% 'Somewhat free' / 'Completely free'

Table 27 Students' perception of supply of freedoms index by university

University	Mean	N valid	Std.Dev.
Cape Town	2.31	385	.5879
Dar es Salaam	2.02	380	.6341
Nairobi	1.97	381	.6857

0=perfect unfreedom; 3=perfect freedom

4.4 Students as transformative democrats?

Throughout this chapter it has been shown that students at the Universities of Cape Town, Dar es Salaam and Nairobi emerge with somewhat different perceptions of the way their country is governed than the mass publics of their respective countries. UON students are generally convinced of the *undemocratic* nature of Kenyan government, and therefore most *dissatisfied* with the way democracy works in their country, but cautiously aware that there still is a considerable level of freedoms availed to them. The students at UDSM also tend to be more critical of the democratic content of Tanzanian government than their fellow citizens. This is quite in contrast to the students at UCT, who seem to live in a '*democratic bubble*' in that they perceive South Africa to be freer than most of their fellow citizens, and are more satisfied with the way democracy works in that country than South Africans in general or their age peers without higher education. It would perhaps be worthwhile exploring whether the South African democracy works better for UCT students than for their educationally and otherwise less privileged peers. That the Cape Town students are slightly more critical of the extent to which SA is a democracy than the mass sample may be due to their much higher demand for democracy (as shown previously).

In the following section we take the notion of 'critical citizenship' a step further and investigate what students' demand for democracy and their perceptions of the supply of democracy might spell for democratic consolidation in their respective countries. In this respect, rather than asking whether they are critical of current regime performance, their evaluation of the current regime will be analysed in relation to different aspects of their demand.

4.4.1 Demand/Supply and regime consolidation

Democratic consolidation has been defined as a phase in the transition from non-democratic rule to democratic rule. As noted in chapter 1, a new democracy is considered to be consolidated once its rules have become accepted by key political actors and its procedures and norms become part of popular political culture. In Linz and Stepan's terms, a democracy is consolidated when it has become 'the only game in town' (1996 in Mattes *et al.* 1999).

A test of democratic consolidation suggested by Huntington (1991) is whether a regime has managed two peaceful transfers of power by means of elections. Taking this basic criterion, none of the three countries in this study can be considered a 'consolidated democracy'. Both, Tanzania and South Africa have experienced dominant party politics since the establishment of electoral, multi-party democracy in the 1990s. Kenya, in contrast, has experienced one peaceful transfer of power in 2002, but in 2007/2008 a serious crisis erupted as election results emerged that could have involved a second transfer of power. Eventually, a transitional government emerged that involved all parties. Thus, using Huntington's criterion, democracy in all three countries is not fully consolidated. Similarly, international democracy rating agencies such as the Economist Intelligence Unit do not consider any of the three countries as fully-fledged democracies, while Freedom

CHAPTER 4 STUDENTS' PERCEPTION OF THE SUPPLY OF DEMOCRACY AND DEMOCRATIC CONSOLIDATION

House only considers South Africa, from among the three, an electoral democracy as per its definition (Puddington 2009).

The micro-foundations of democratic consolidation are to be found in the political attitudes and behaviours of citizens (as Mattes *et al.* 1999 and Schmidt 1996 suggest). In order to assess the extent to which students consider democracy in their country to be consolidated, we apply a model of regime consolidation based on the work of Mattes and others (1999). In terms of this model, we conceptualise regime consolidation as *at equilibrium between demand for democracy and perceived supply of democracy* in a country (*compare* Mattes *et al.* 1999: 28–29). Our findings are then compared with the most recent mass public data (and model of regime consolidation of Bratton and Mattes 2009); they are further corroborated with students' responses to other questions in the Student Governance Survey. The overall quest is to determine whether the future educated elite of Kenya, Tanzania and South Africa, as represented by students of the premier universities in these countries, may be counted among the pro-democratic forces in their country, that is, whether they are impatient, critical democrats or as we call them, transformative democrats.

4.4.2 Democratic consolidation in comparative perspective

Considering the survey findings of students' demand for democracy and perceived supply of democracy in tandem, it is possible to construct a complex picture of regime consolidation in Kenya, South Africa and Tanzania from a student perspective. Table 28 summarises the findings of the two foregoing chapters. It shows that student demand for democracy is highest in South Africa (UCT), followed by Kenya (UON) and Tanzania (UDSM). It further shows students' perception of the supply of democracy indicating differences in perceived regime performance in the three countries. Again, UCT students rate their country the highest, followed by UDSM and UON students.

Table 28 Students' expressed demand and perceived supply of democracy and freedom

	Kenya	South Africa	Tanzania
Demand			
Preference for democracy*	70	72	65
Rejection of non-democratic alternatives^	89	90	82
Demand for freedoms**	72	81	67
Supply			
Country is a democracy^^	11	61	39
Satisfied with regime performance***	13	57	30
Supply of freedoms^^^	70	86	71

* % Always prefer democracy. ^ % Average of three items measuring rejection of non-democratic alternatives.
** % Average of six items measuring support for political freedoms. ^^ % Average of two items measuring freeness and fairness of elections and perception of extent to which the country is a democracy. *** % Fairly/Very satisfied with democracy; ^^^ % Average of three items measuring perceived supply of political freedoms.

The relationship between students' expressed demand for, and perceived supply of corresponding regime features is strikingly illustrated in Figure 22 (below; as per values in Table 28). The extent of equilibrium/disequilibrium between corresponding features provides a striking picture of the extent to which students perceive their demand for

Figure 22 Regime consolidation from the student perspective

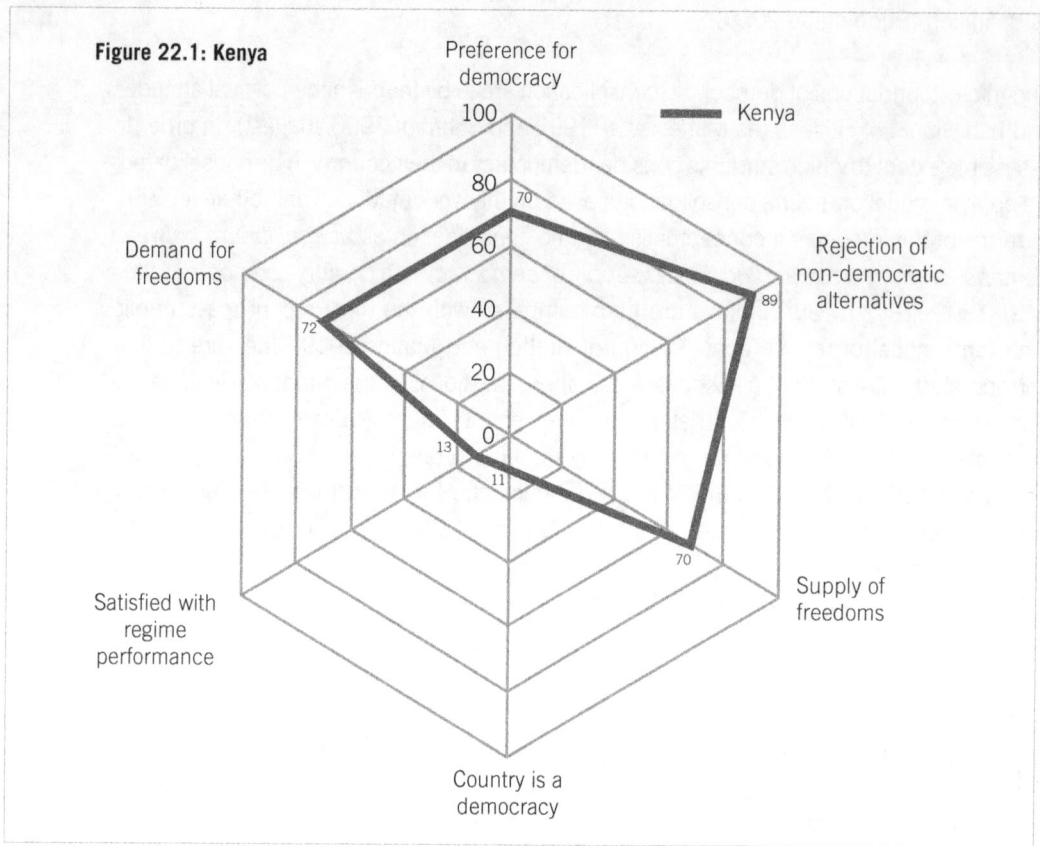

Figure 22.1: Kenya

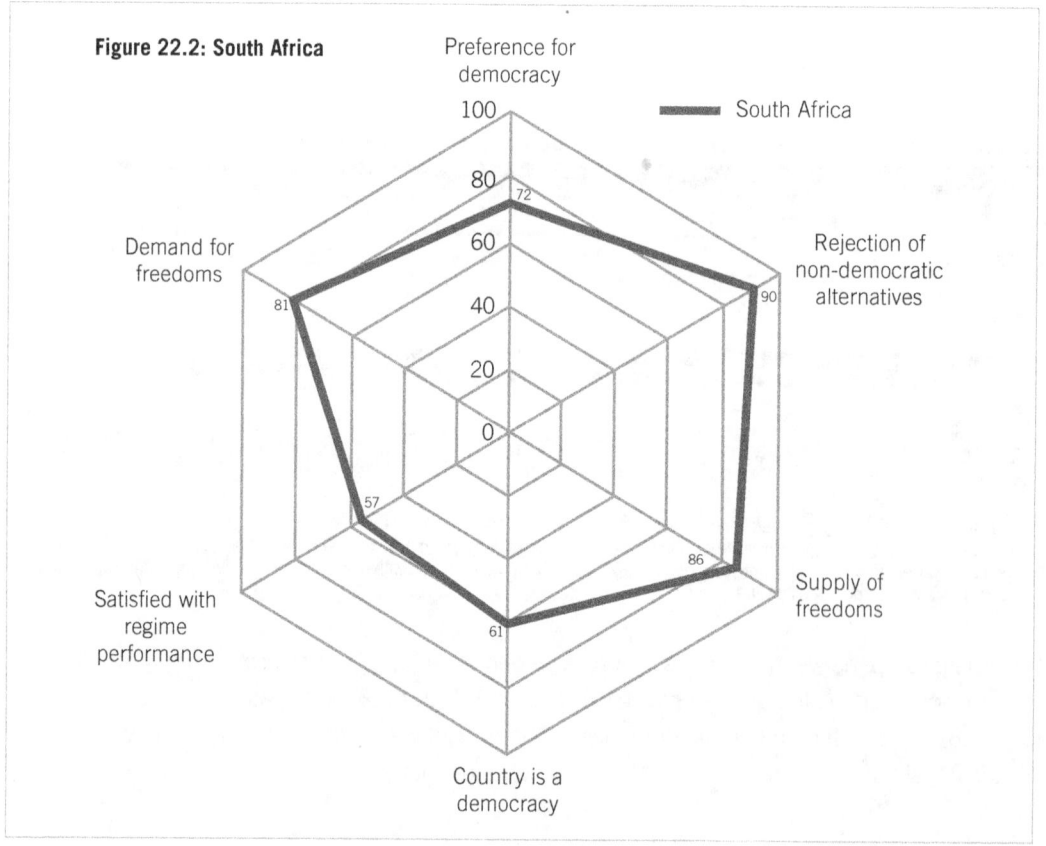

Figure 22.2: South Africa

Figure 22 Regime consolidation from the student perspective (cont.)

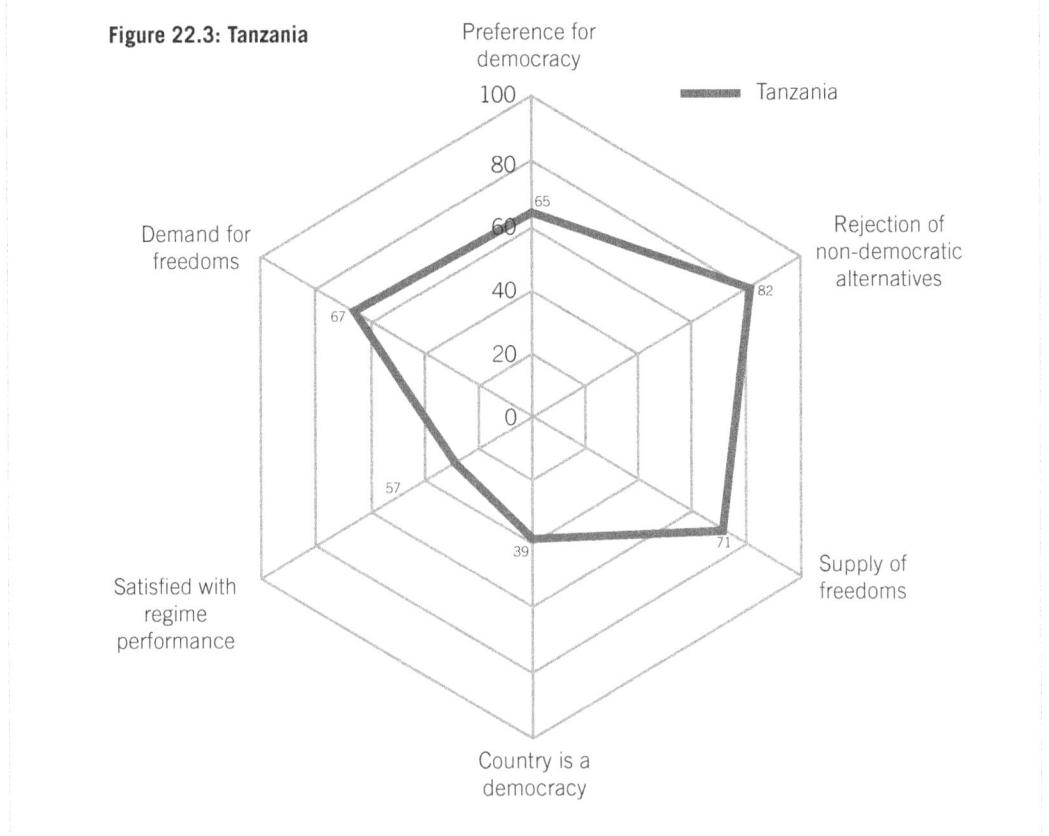

democracy to have been met by the current political system. In this regard, the picture can be interpreted in terms of the consolidation of the current political regime *as a democracy* in the eyes of students, considering the extent to which features inherent in the current regime are considered to live up to (or fail to live up to) the democratic aspirations of students. Thus, while equilibrium of demand and supply indicates regime consolidation, a modest disequilibrium can be interpreted as student ambiguity towards the current regime and a certain reform potential, while a severe disequilibrium harbours potential for regime change.

Figure 22.1 illustrates a severe *disequilibrium* between the expressed demand for democracy and students' perception of regime performance in Kenya. Only the supply of political freedoms is somewhat in equilibrium with students' expressed demand (and at a level comparable to TZN/SA) suggesting a liberalised rather than democratic political system. Apart from that, regime performance in Kenya – measured in terms of freeness and fairness of election, satisfaction with the current regime, and evaluation of the extent of democracy of the country – is evaluated very low. This results in a situation where a great majority of students at the University of Nairobi longs for democracy, but do not think they are receiving it. In terms of our model, the severe disequilibrium harbours potential for pro-democratic regime change in Kenya. Fast steps towards fulfilling this potential for change occurred in 2010 as a new constitution was adopted in a plebiscite that has the potential of ushering in a new democratic chapter in Kenya's political history. UON students may well be the kind of transformative democrats needed to make this happen; Figure 15 (above) indicates that they are likely to find very fertile ground among fellow Kenyans for pro-democratic ideas and action.

In South Africa, UCT students have even slightly higher expectations of democratic governance than in Kenya; but at the same time, they also think that they actually get a good share of it. The demand and supply model provides a picture of a relative *equilibrium* of student demand for, and perceived supply of, freedom and democracy in South Africa. A majority of students at UCT think that their strong preference for democracy is largely satisfied by the way the country is governed. Moreover, the supply of political freedoms actually marginally outstrips students' expressed demand (see Figure 22.2). Thus, most UCT students are likely to be complacent about democracy at present; but their widespread high demand for democracy may turn the majority of student leaders and activists (especially those who are also committed democrats, see Table 20 and Table 21) into a pro-democratic transformative force, should they perceive the supply of democracy to be under threat (as seen, for instance, in students' march against corruption in 2009). They would, however, not likely find majority support in the South African public or among their age cohort for such a pro-democratic cause (compare Figure 15).

The Tanzanian model (Figure 22.3) shows a noticeable *disequilibrium,* albeit not as severe as in the Kenyan case. On the one hand, student demand for democracy in Tanzania is lower than in the other two countries (but still about two-thirds of the students prefer democracy and four-fifths reject its non-democratic alternatives). On the other hand, about two-thirds are also dissatisfied with the supply of democracy and regime performance in Tanzania. Only the supply of political freedoms lives up to (and actually exceeds) students' expectations. The Tanzanian model suggests reform potential in a polity that is perceived as liberalised but not democratised; and yet, the thrust is not clearly towards democracy. Moreover, provided that only about a third of the UDSM students are truly committed democrats (see Figure 15), students' role in pro-democratic change is likely to be limited to a small core of transformative democrats. Unless the committed democrats in the student body can politically educate and mobilise their peers as well as connect with the committed democrats from off-campus, division in the student body, ambiguity and complacency will frustrate students' potential contribution to pro-democratic transformation and consolidation.

Comparing the findings from the Student Governance Survey and its model of democratic consolidation with the Afrobarometer data and the Bratton and Mattes model (2009) provides further insights. The Afrobarometer model of regime consolidation is also based on the demand/supply model, but it excludes demand/supply of freedoms (Bratton & Mattes 2009). In this model, and using mass public data, South Africa is perceived to be consolidating as a hybrid democracy; while Kenya and Tanzania both feature as unconsolidated regimes, albeit for different reasons. In Kenya the mass public (like the UON students) demand more democracy than the political elites are willing to supply, while in Tanzania, the political regime seems to provide more democracy than the mass public actually demands (which is contrary to the UDSM student survey findings).

4.4.3 Give the regime more time or revolution?

A final way of considering the potential for deepening democratic consolidation and students' potential role therein is to consider their willingness to give the existing political system more time to live up to students' expectations. This research question is provided for by a set of indicators in the Student Governance Survey that directly measure students' support for regime change.

Students are asked to agree/disagree with the statements *'Our present system of elected government should be given more time to deal with inherited problems'* and *'If our present system does not produce results soon, we should try another form of government'*. In the original Afrobarometer survey, these statements are considered as mutually exclusive questions, indicating support for democracy. For our purposes, we take them more literally as indicators of support for the *existing regime* (however conceived) whereby the emphasis in the first question is on *giving more time* while in the second question it is on *trying another regime type.* Figure 23 and Figure 24 summarise students' responses in this regard.

Figure 23 Students' willingness to give the present system more time

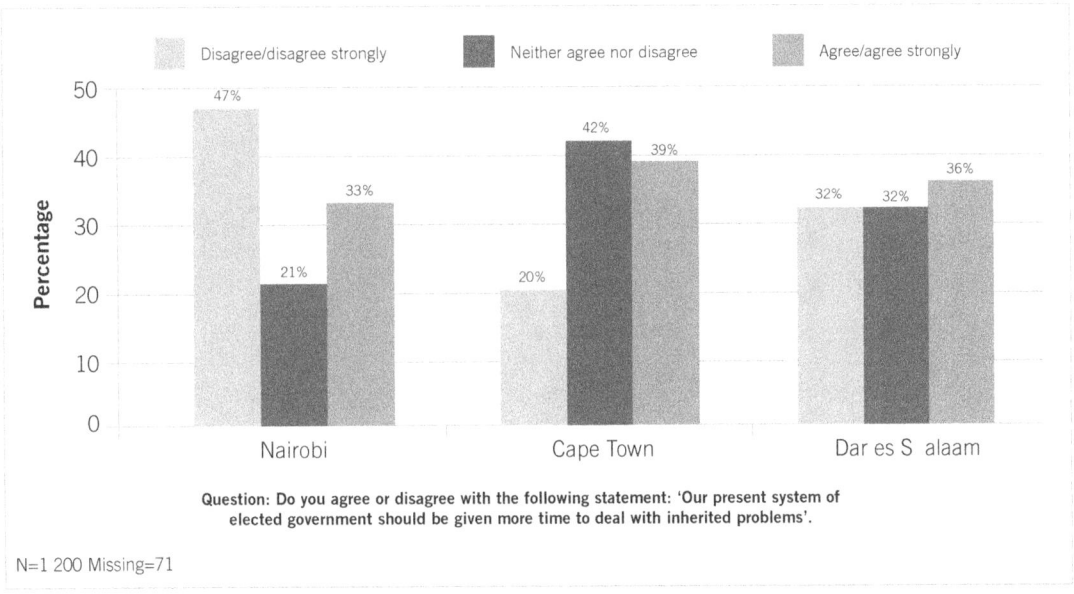

Question: Do you agree or disagree with the following statement: 'Our present system of elected government should be given more time to deal with inherited problems'.

N=1 200 Missing=71

Both, Figure 23 and Figure 24 confirm the extent of dissatisfaction that students at the University of Nairobi have with the current political regime. Around half of the students from UON long for regime change with just over half (52%) 'agreeing or strongly agreeing' that they should try another form of government and the balance (47%) stating that they do not consider that their present system should be given more time. Conversely, only between a quarter and a third of the UON students express support for the transitional dispensation in Kenya and are prepared to give it more time.

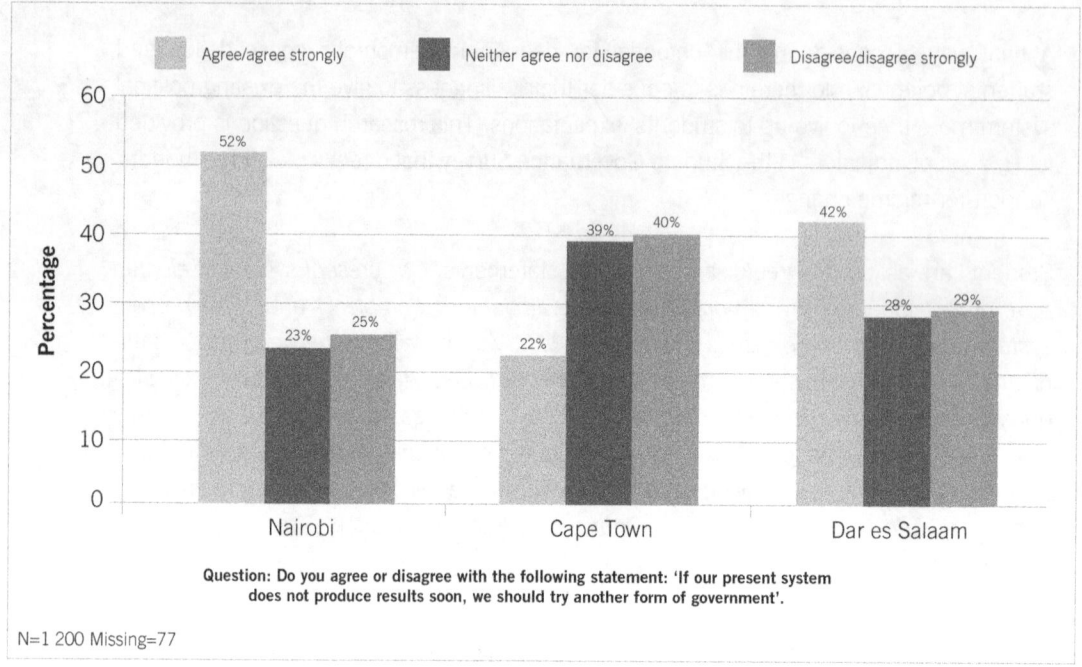

Figure 24 Students' willingness to try another form of government

Question: Do you agree or disagree with the following statement: 'If our present system does not produce results soon, we should try another form of government'.

N=1 200 Missing=77

The disequilibrium between demand for democracy and supply of democracy in Kenya (identified above Figure 22.1) produces a large group of students at UON that are not only dissatisfied with the current regime but also *impatient* for regime change. When looking at this group more closely it shows that marginally more student leaders are impatient for change (54%) than students not in leadership (46%); and more student leaders are prepared to try another form of government (53%) than students not in leadership (51%). From the student perspective, there is certainly pro-democratic transformation potential in Kenya.

In Tanzania the political situation is very different from that in Kenya. Since the re-establishment of multi-party democracy in the 1990s (indeed since independence), the same political party, that is CCM, has been dominating the political sphere. As shown above, the UDSM students are in the strange position that they demand more democracy than the political system is supplying, while the Tanzanian public in general gets more democracy than it actually wants. Responses to the statements about regime continuation or regime change receive no student majorities, reflecting at once neither clear support nor clear opposition towards the current system.

As may be expected from the foregoing analyses, the students at UCT emerge again as the most supportive of the current political system in their country. As the relative equilibrium in the demand/supply models of both student and mass sample suggest, there is little willingness among students to consider regime change. Given the chance, only about a fifth of the respondents would be in favour of trying out something else. They are outnumbered, however, by almost double the number of students who are in favour of giving the current régime more time to deal with inherited problems and who oppose trying out a different system of government, and another two-fifths who are indifferent to the question. Thus, student support for the current political dispensation in South Africa comes in a context where a sizeable group (almost equal in size to the supporters of the current regime), are indifferent towards the question.

4.4.4 Transformative citizenship by university

The notion of 'transformative democrats' pursued in this section defines those respondents who have consistently high demand for democracy in that they *always prefer democracy*, they are *critical or highly critical of the extent of democracy* in their country, and they are *impatient for regime change*. These three requirements, which are measured by three different indicators in the questionnaire, represent a rather stringent set of requirements.[17]

Figure 25 Transformative democrats: impatient, critical, democratic

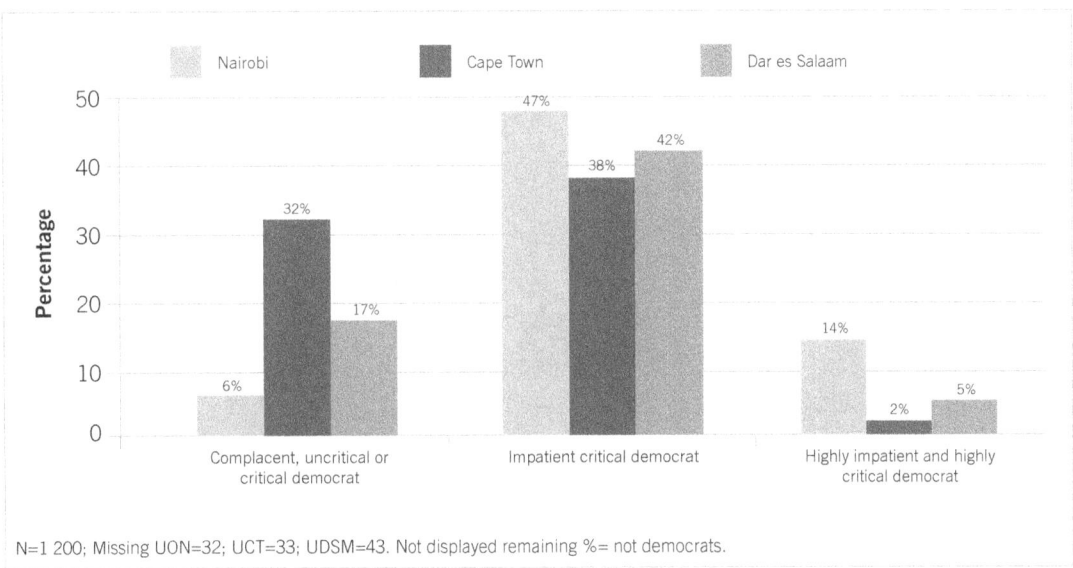

N=1 200; Missing UON=32; UCT=33; UDSM=43. Not displayed remaining %= not democrats.

Figure 25 shows the extent to which the Universities of Cape Town, Dar es Salaam and Nairobi educate a potential resource of transformative democrats. As may be expected, the students at UON top the list: 61% of the UON students are critical democrats who are impatient to see regime change in their country. 14% thereof are even highly impatient and highly critical. The picture at UDSM is somewhat similar but less extreme than that at UON. Here just less than half of the students can be described as transformative democrats, while a sizable number of students (17%) are democrats who are fairly happy and not impatient with the current regime. Lastly, the group of pro-democratic, regime critical, impatient students is smallest at the University of Cape Town. Moreover, there are very few among the students surveyed at UCT who are highly impatient for regime change and highly critical of the present dispensation. Rather, as was to be expected, almost a

---

17 Thus, the democratic commitment of transformative democrats is not necessarily as exclusive as that of committed democrats. Transformative democrats while they say they always prefer democracy will not necessarily always reject all non-democratic alternatives.

third of UCT students are happily content democrats who see no need for further political transformation.

4.4.5 Transformative citizenship in national comparative perspective

In the national perspective, the students of all three universities turn out to be significantly more likely to be transformative democrats than their fellow citizens. In particular, students tend to be much more impatient with the ability of the current regime to produce results, and also more critical of national government (except in the UCT case study) than their less educated age cohort and the public at large (see Figure 26).

Figure 26 Transformative democrats in comparative perspective

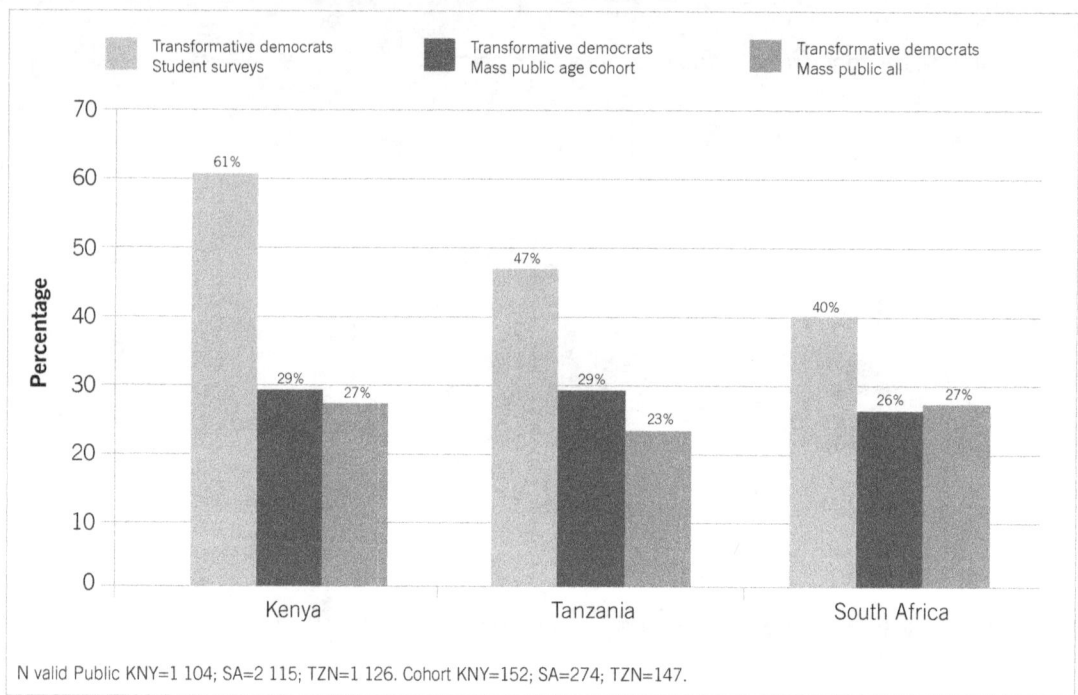

N valid Public KNY=1 104; SA=2 115; TZN=1 126. Cohort KNY=152; SA=274; TZN=147.

The students of the University of Nairobi are not only the most likely transformative democrats among the three university samples, but also in the context of Kenyan public opinion. This is mostly because the students are by far more *impatient* for democratic transformation than their age peers without higher education and the Kenyan public at large. A striking feature of the Kenyan mass sample is precisely the large number of *complacent* and relatively *uncritical* democrats (46% of general sample; 38% of age cohort) that make up the remainder.

UDSM students are also much more likely to be transformative democrats than Tanzanians in general; however, the UDSM transformative democrats are neither as highly critical nor as highly impatient as UON students. Insofar they are closer to Tanzanians in general of whom the majority see no urgency for regime transformation (61%) and are *uncritical* of the limited democracy it offers (51%).

In the national comparative perspective, the three South African samples are closest to each other on the question of transformative citizenship. Like UDSM students, UCT's transformative democrats are neither highly critical nor highly impatient; their longing for regime transformation must really be interpreted as a commitment to a deepening of the existing democracy. The same accounts for the mass sample. In addition, over a third of South Africans in general and of the 20–23 age cohort are fairly regime-critical democrats who see, however, no urgency in 'trying another form of government'.

4.5   Summary and conclusion

This chapter has considered students' perception of the supply of democracy in their country, and analysed students' responses in terms of the different models of democratic consolidation and the related notion of transformative citizenship. It has shown that students are more likely to evaluate the performance of democracy in their country critically than their fellow citizens. More especially, the comparative perspective using Afrobarometer data shows that the views of the respective age cohorts (without higher education) in the mass sample tends to be closer to the general view than to those of the students. In the UON and UDSM cases, student views are typically more critical of regime performance than those of the mass publics, while in the South African case, UCT students perceive the political system typically as more satisfactory and freer than their fellow citizens.

The chapter shows that UON students are generally convinced of the *undemocratic* nature of Kenyan government, and therefore most *dissatisfied* with the way democracy works in their country, but cautiously aware that there still is a considerable level of freedoms availed to them. Similarly, the students at UDSM also tend to be more critical of the democratic content of Tanzanian government than their fellow citizens. This is quite in contrast to the students at UCT who perceive South Africa to be freer than most of their fellow citizens, and are more satisfied with the way democracy works in their country than South Africans in general or their age peers without higher education.

Using a demand/supply model of democratic consolidation illustrates the disparities between the students' demand for democracy and their perception of what they are getting. If an equilibrium between demand and supply is conceptualised as a measure of regime consolidation, Kenya emerges as ready for pro-democratic regime change from a student perspective, while students consider Tanzanian democracy in need of reform and further deepening. In contrast, UCT students perceive South Africa as fairly consolidated at a level of democracy that the majority can agree with, albeit within a context of consistently high student demand for democracy.

In order to consider whether students may emerge within their respective contexts of regime consolidation as a pro-democratic transformative force to be reckoned with, student views have been analysed in terms of the notion of 'transformative democrat'. The notion of transformative democrat characterises those students who *always prefer democracy*, are *critical of the current extent of democracy* in their country, and *impatient for regime change* in that they are ready to try something else. It emerges that almost two-thirds of UON students would readily support democratic transformation in their country, while under half at UDSM (47%) and only 40% at UCT would do the same (whereby less students at UDSM and UCT feel as strongly about this as UON students). It also shows that a rather large group of UCT students who are democrats do not see the need for any urgent and drastic change in the South African political system. The key difference between students and the mass samples in this respect has been that students tend to be more *impatient* and *critical* (especially UON; to a lesser extent UDSM) or *more democratically inclined* (UCT) than their fellow citizens.

Overall the chapter therefore shows that students' perception of the supply of democracy in Kenya and Tanzania is such that a majority would support pro-democratic change. Neither Kenya nor Tanzania can be considered consolidated democracies from the student perspective. In this regard, the findings of the Student Governance Surveys thus concur with international democracy ratings. Indeed, many of the young and upcoming citizens who are being educated at UON and UDSM are eager to see democratic changes in their country (even if not all of them are consistently committed democrats – as chapter 3 shows). Especially among the students at the University of Nairobi, there is a vast majority of transformative democrats who are critical of the way government works in their country and impatient for seeing change.

After having investigated students' demand for democracy and their perceptions of the supply of democratic governance in their respective countries in relation to the notions of 'commitment to democracy' and 'transformative citizenship', the report now turns to investigate the idea of 'active citizenship' or the ways by which students actually seek to act on their commitments to democracy and the deepening of democracy in their country.

Chapter 5
Students' Political Engagement and Behaviour

Keeping in mind students' understandings of democracy, which chiefly involve conceptions of participatory decision-making in a liberal-democratic polity and their high demand for democracy, as well as the findings of the previous chapter that highlighted students' perception of the supply of democracy in their own countries, this chapter looks at the way students actively participate in the political realm as observers, potential actors, and actual actors. Are students interested in and regularly discussing politics? How do they access information about politics? Do they know about political incumbents and institutions in their country (and on their campus)? In what way do students participate in politics? Do students participate in elections? Are there other forms of civic participation in which students engage, like attending political meetings, contacting officials, or protesting on or off campus? This chapter considers responses from the survey to these and related questions.

First, however, it is incumbent to ask whether students actually consider it appropriate for themselves to participate in politics. As part of the survey, students were asked to consider the statement, '*University students should concentrate on their studies and not become involved in politics*'. Less than 10% of respondents agree with it outright. Rather almost two-thirds disagree or strongly disagree with the proposition that students should stay out of politics (N valid=1 130). The corresponding question whether students should therefore '*Examine and criticize government on behalf of the less privileged in the country*' finds accordingly overwhelming support (75% 'strongly agree'/'agree' vs. 7% 'disagree'/'strongly disagree'; rest: 'undecided') (N valid=1 129). When looking at the responses by university it shows that support for the involvement of students in politics is strongest among students at UDSM and least strong (but still supported by over two-thirds) at UCT.

5.1 Students' cognitive engagement with politics

In order for students to be able to successfully participate in politics on and off campus, they need to be cognitively engaged and aware of public affairs and politics around them. Awareness of politics has presumably many dimensions. In the survey, cognitive awareness is measured in terms of engaging with politics on a regular basis as an interest and discussion topic, making frequent use of news media and knowing key political incumbents and institutions.

5.1.1 Interest in politics and media use

There is considerable student interest in politics across all campuses. At UCT, 75% of respondents say that they are 'somewhat/very interested' in politics and government. At UON and UDSM this respective share is 70% and 69% (compare Table 29).

Table 29 Interest in public affairs (politics and government)

	University			Total
	Nairobi	Cape Town	Dar es Salaam	
Not interested at all	8%	4%	8%	7%
Not very interested	23%	22%	23%	22%
Somewhat/very interested	70%	75%	69%	71%

Question: 'How interested are you in public affairs (especially in politics and government)?'
N=1 200 Missing=2

While the student figures are well above the African average (64%) of expressed interest in politics, they are not particularly high within the context of Tanzanian and Kenyan mass public data. Thus, UON students follow their comparatively high national average of 72%. In contrast, the students at UDSM seem actually less interested in politics than the average Tanzanian or their comparative age cohort without higher education. In 2008, 83% of Tanzanians expressed great interest in politics, giving it the highest level of interest of all surveyed African countries (Gyimah-Boadi & Armah Attoh 2009). Lastly, considering that interest in politics in South Africa at 55% is below the African average, and that only half of the South African age cohort express interest in public affairs and politics, the level of political interest among UCT students is extraordinarily high at 75% (see Figure 27).

Figure 27 Student interest in politics in comparative perspective

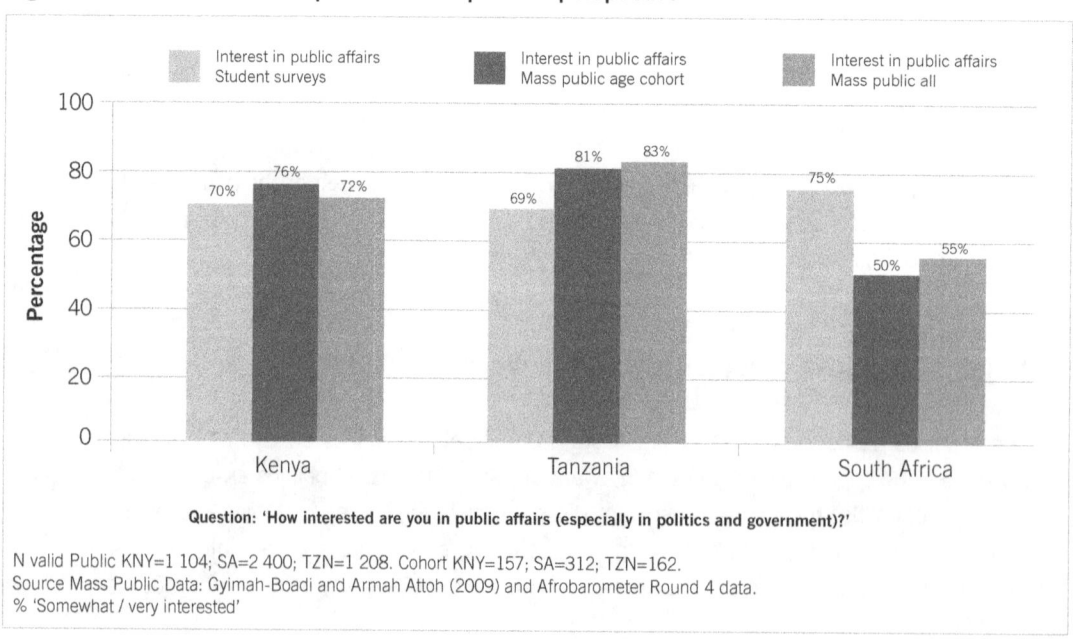

Question: 'How interested are you in public affairs (especially in politics and government)?'

N valid Public KNY=1 104; SA=2 400; TZN=1 208. Cohort KNY=157; SA=312; TZN=162.
Source Mass Public Data: Gyimah-Boadi and Armah Attoh (2009) and Afrobarometer Round 4 data.
% 'Somewhat / very interested'

When students are asked how often they actually discuss politics with friends and family, their frequency of discussion seems to actually outperform their interest in public affairs. About a third of the students on each campus say they discuss political matters 'frequently'; just under two-thirds say they do so at least 'occasionally'. The figures of those saying they avoid the topic altogether are negligible at all three universities (compare Table 30).

Table 30 Frequency of discussing politics

	University			Total
	Nairobi	Cape Town	Dar es Salaam	
Never	4%	6%	5%	5%
Occasionally	62%	62%	61%	62%
Frequently	34%	33%	34%	33%

Question: 'When you get together with fellow students, friends or family, do you discuss political matters?'
N=1 200 Missing=3

In contrast, the respective national averages are somewhat lower. Thus, while at UON those who say they discuss politics 'occasionally'/'frequently' make up 96%, the Kenya-wide figure is only 79%. Similarly at UDSM, 95% of students discuss politics regularly while as in Kenya 79% of the Tanzanian public in general does so. The UCT figure of 95% is extraordinarily high for South Africa. Only two-thirds of the South African public discuss politics regularly with friends and family (see Figure 28).

Figure 28 Frequency of students discussing politics in comparative perspective

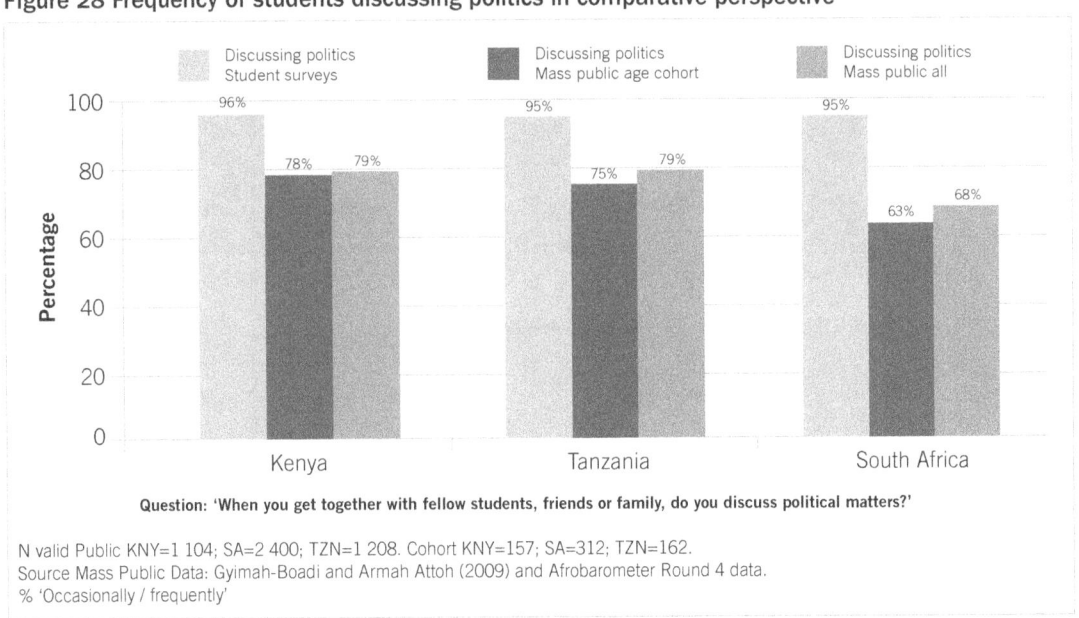

Question: 'When you get together with fellow students, friends or family, do you discuss political matters?'
N valid Public KNY=1 104; SA=2 400; TZN=1 208. Cohort KNY=157; SA=312; TZN=162.
Source Mass Public Data: Gyimah-Boadi and Armah Attoh (2009) and Afrobarometer Round 4 data.
% 'Occasionally / frequently'

The Student Governance Surveys therefore find that the proportion of students who discuss politics frequently is high on all three campuses – almost 30% above the African average and well above the national averages as well. Considering this in relation to students' expressed interest in politics, it appears that student life may offer advantages to the politically interested: The topic of politics is more often discussed than perhaps all students would like!

A related question to that of students' interest in and discussion of politics is where students get their news from. Figure 29 and Figure 31 (below) show that radio and TV are the news sources most frequently used by most students. Four-fifths of the students say that they use these sources either daily or several times a week to inform themselves about the latest news. In addition, newspaper use and internet use are also highly prevalent. Two-thirds of students say they read newspapers and/or internet news sites daily or almost daily (see Figure 30 and Figure 32 below).

Comparing the Student Governance Surveys with Afrobarometer data shows that students have great advantages of access to certain news sources over the public in general and their age peers who are not at university. Except for radio, which is most widely accessible and used daily or several times a week, access to and use of other news media is skewed in favour of students (Figure 29).

Figure 29 Use of radio

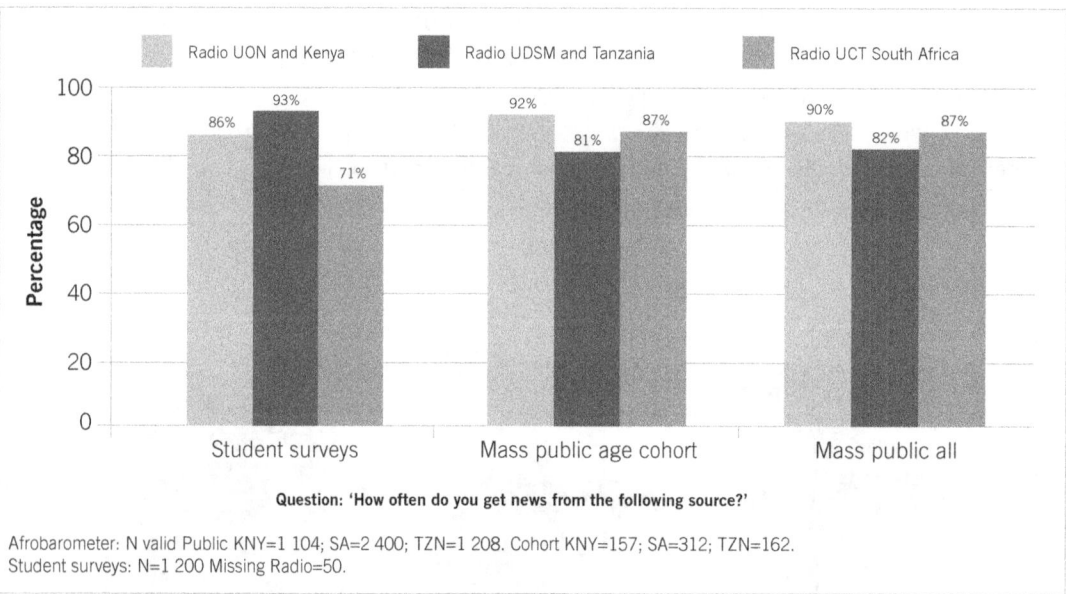

Question: 'How often do you get news from the following source?'

Afrobarometer: N valid Public KNY=1 104; SA=2 400; TZN=1 208. Cohort KNY=157; SA=312; TZN=162.
Student surveys: N=1 200 Missing Radio=50.

Thus, UON students are twice as likely as their age cohort at large to use newspapers daily or several times a week; UDSM students are three times as likely. Only in South Africa is access to newspapers evenly distributed (at just over 50% for all samples) (see Figure 30).

The East African students are also far more likely to use TV as a source of news than their fellow citizens. UCT students, in contrast, don't seem to use TV as often as their fellow citizens or the students in Nairobi and Dar es Salaam (compare Figure 31).

Thus, while there is already a significant disparity in use of TV and newspapers between students and the public at large in Kenya and Tanzania (but not so in South Africa), the strongest impact of the university environment on access to news comes with the internet.

CHAPTER 5 STUDENTS' POLITICAL ENGAGEMENT AND BEHAVIOUR

Figure 30 Use of newspapers

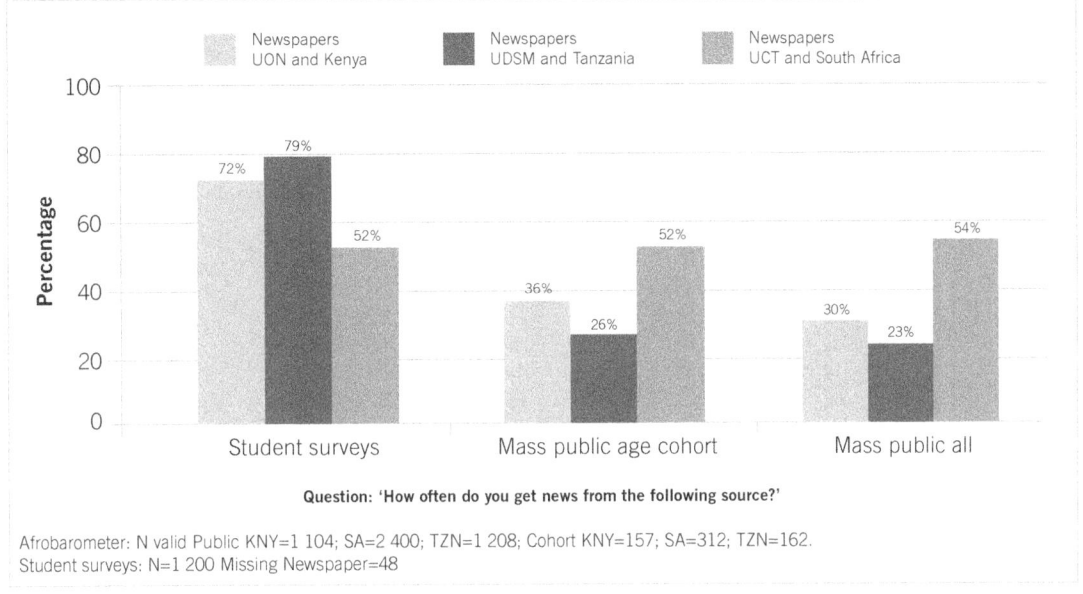

Question: 'How often do you get news from the following source?'

Afrobarometer: N valid Public KNY=1 104; SA=2 400; TZN=1 208; Cohort KNY=157; SA=312; TZN=162.
Student surveys: N=1 200 Missing Newspaper=48

Figure 31 Use of TV

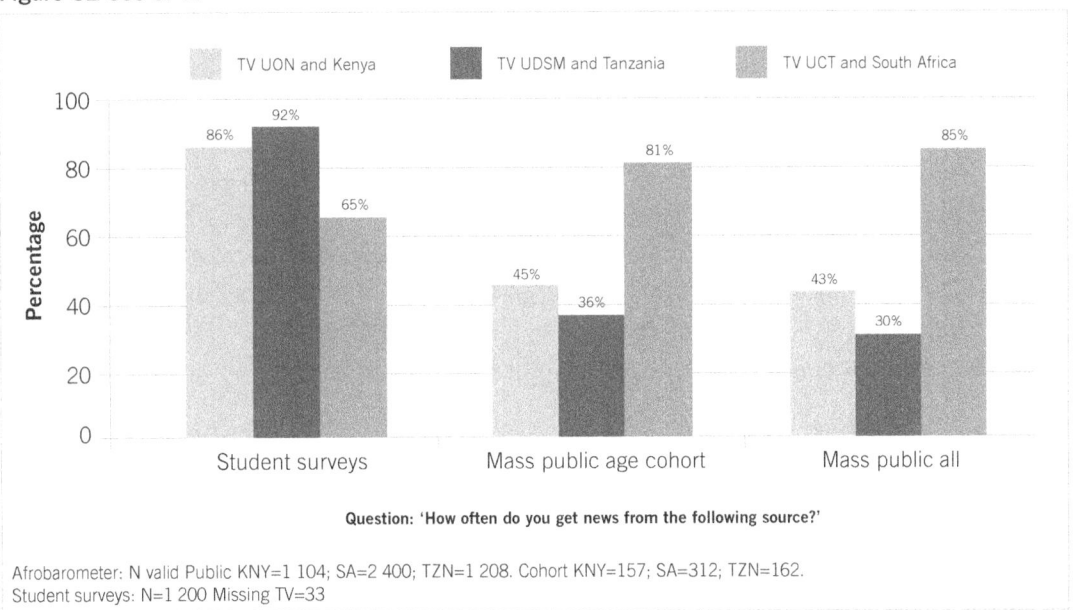

Question: 'How often do you get news from the following source?'

Afrobarometer: N valid Public KNY=1 104; SA=2 400; TZN=1 208. Cohort KNY=157; SA=312; TZN=162.
Student surveys: N=1 200 Missing TV=33

While the vast majority of students on all three campuses say they use the internet daily or several times a week (between 85% and 88%), use of the internet is minimal among the population in general (between 1% and 10%). As Figure 32 illustrates, the internet is also not a typical 'youth' medium; rather it is a medium to which students have special access through the universities. Ismail and Graham (2009) show that even when measured at a lesser, monthly frequency mass publics still do not have access to the internet to the extent that students do (i.e. use of internet by mass publics at least once a month: Kenya 15%; Tanzania 3%; South Africa 19%).

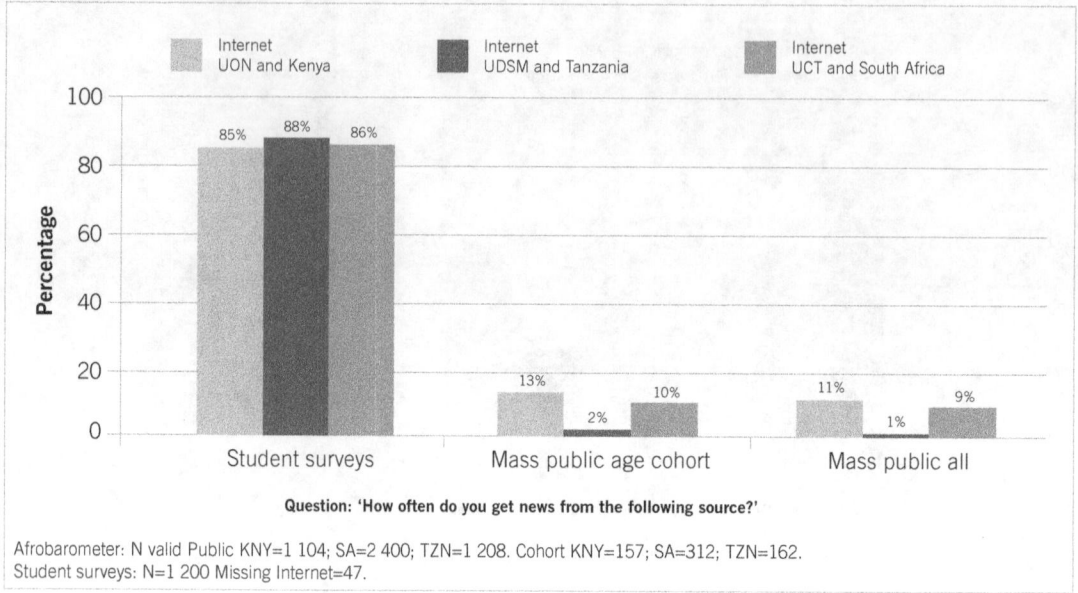

Figure 32 Use of internet

Question: 'How often do you get news from the following source?'

Afrobarometer: N valid Public KNY=1 104; SA=2 400; TZN=1 208. Cohort KNY=157; SA=312; TZN=162.
Student surveys: N=1 200 Missing Internet=47.

It appears therefore that in terms of news media and thus access to information about public affairs and politics, the Universities of Dar es Salaam and Nairobi put students at a distinct advantage compared to the Tanzanian and Kenyan publics in general and compared to the students' age peers who are not at university. In this respect, these universities provide a privileged place for the politically interested citizen. In Cape Town, by contrast, the situation is far less marked. Even though students are more interested in public affairs than South Africans in general and discuss politics more frequently, their use of radio and TV (but not newspapers) is less frequent than the general public or their age cohort. The internet has seemingly already eclipsed radio and TV as news media at UCT.

5.1.2 Knowledge about politics

Having seen the high levels of students' engagement with politics and use of news media, the question now is whether this interest in public affairs and wealth of information also translates into basic knowledge about politics. Can students correctly identify political incumbents on campus and in national government? Do they know the basics about the institutions that govern the university and the nation?

Table 31 Political knowledge: correctly naming incumbents

	University			Total
	Nairobi	Cape Town	Dar es Salaam	
Dean of Students/ Executive Director of Student Affairs	52%	7%	27%	28%
President of Student Union/SRC	82%	30%	62%	58%
Vice-Chancellor	83%	69%	80%	77%
Minister of Finance	96%	55%	60%	71%
Your Member of Parliament	87%	n/a[1]	70%	68%
President of the Country	98%	95%	99%	97%

Question: 'Can you tell me the name of...' %= correct answer; N= 1 200 Missing Dean=50; Missing President SU=69; Missing VC=18; Missing Minister=52; Missing MP=52; Missing President=30.

CHAPTER 5 STUDENTS' POLITICAL ENGAGEMENT AND BEHAVIOUR

With regard to political incumbents at national level, the survey asked students to identify the name of the president, their member of parliament, and the minister of finance. At university level, the question was asked about the name of the president of the student union or SRC, the vice-chancellor of the university, and the dean of students.

Table 31 shows that virtually all students know the name of the president of their country. That is, however, where the similarities end. By far the most knowledgeable about political incumbents – both on and off campus are the students of the University of Nairobi. Vast majorities of UON students can correctly identify the minister of finance by name (96%), their member of parliament (87%), as well as the vice-chancellor of their university (83%) and the president of the student union (82%). Still over half know the name of the dean of students at UON.

At the University of Dar es Salaam, there is still a large majority who can correctly identify their MP (70%) and the minister of finance of Tanzania (60%), as well as at university level the vice-chancellor of UDSM (80%) and student president of the USRC (62%).[18] However, only just over a quarter of the students know the name of their dean of students.

From the three groups, the students of the University of Cape Town emerge as the least knowledgeable about political incumbents and campus officials. The vast majority (95%) can correctly name the president of the Republic of South Africa and just over half know the name of the minister of finance (55%). The name of their vice-chancellor is known by 69% of the students, but only 30% know the UCT SRC president by name and a tiny minority (7%) can identify the executive director of student affairs correctly.

Taking the question about the minister of finance as an example in the national comparative perspective shows that the UON and UDSM students are much more knowledgeable about this specific political incumbent than their compatriots. Compared to only 12% of Tanzanians, 60% of UDSM students correctly name the minister of finance; in Kenya, where on average 44% of Afrobarometer respondents get the minister's name right, it is 96% of the UON students. In South Africa, in contrast, 76% of South Africans identified the longstanding and popular minister of finance correctly in the 2008 Afrobarometer survey, that is, significantly more than the UCT students. However, while the survey was conducted at UCT a new cabinet was under formation and thus some students named (correctly) the still incumbent former minister while others named the new minister as incumbent; moreover, many answered 'know but can't remember'. 55% of UCT students correctly named the former minister or his successor, which, albeit 20% below the national figure of 76%, can be taken under the circumstances as a fair score (Figure 33).

The second dimension of cognitive political awareness measured in the Student Governance Surveys is knowledge about key political institutions. At a general level, the surveys show that students are more knowledgeable about incumbents than institutions and that knowledge about the political institutions at national level is far more prevalent

---

18 In the UDSM case, the name of the last USRC president was accepted (along with the current transitional president of the student union) since he had been rusticated by university management only months before the survey and was considered by many students still as the rightful USRC president.

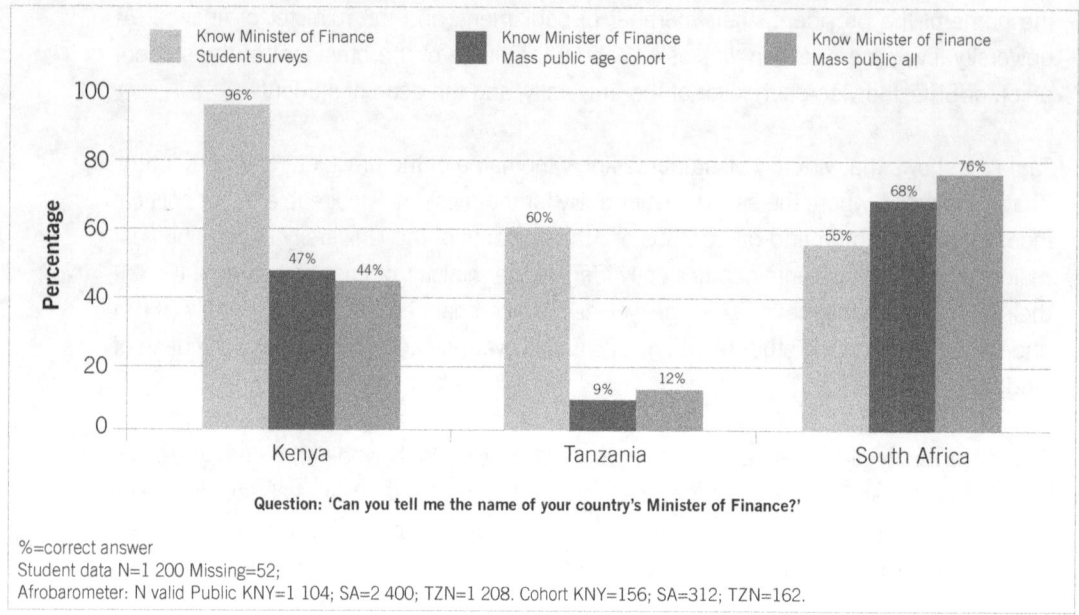

Figure 33 Students naming the finance minister correctly in comparative perspective

Question: 'Can you tell me the name of your country's Minister of Finance?'

%=correct answer
Student data N=1 200 Missing=52;
Afrobarometer: N valid Public KNY=1 104; SA=2 400; TZN=1 208. Cohort KNY=156; SA=312; TZN=162.

among students from all the three campuses than knowledge about university governing bodies. As may be expected, virtually all students can name the majority party that governs in their country correctly. The number of years the president can constitutionally hold office is known by 63% of students at UCT, 72% at UDSM and 84% at UON. The role of the courts in determining the constitutionality of a law is known to half of the students at UCT, but to less than a third of UDSM and UON students.

Table 32 Political knowledge: correctly naming institutions

	University			Total
	Nairobi	Cape Town	Dar es Salaam	
University Governing Body	4%	5%	14%	7%
Main membership of the Senate	6%	5%	17%	9%
Role of Student Representative Body	16%	22%	16%	18%
Presidential term limitation	84%	63%	72%	73%
Role of courts	27%	52%	30%	36%
Majority party	94%	91%	91%	92%

Question: 'Do you happen to know...' %= correct answer
N=1 200 Missing UGB=33; Missing Senate=47; Missing SR=46; Missing MP=35; Missing Pres=49; Missing Courts=55.

With respect to university level institutions, knowledge about governing institutions is scarce. Only between a sixth and a fifth of students know that one of the functions of their student representative body is to appoint representatives to the university's top decision-making bodies, i.e. the Council and Senate. Except at UDSM, where marginally more students are informed about university institutions, Table 32 shows that less than 10% of students at UCT and UON know the basics about the composition of the Senate or which body holds the vice-chancellor accountable.

This section has shown that the university offers in various ways a privileged space for cognitive engagement with politics. It offers a space for more frequent discussion of public affairs and more frequent access to the use of news media (i.e. media of all kinds at UON and UDSM, and especially to the internet at UCT). This has a highly positive influence on the level of knowledge about politics among students at UDSM and UON, but to a lesser extent on students at UCT.[19]

5.2 Students' political participation

Democratic processes require the active participation of citizens above participation in elections to be sustained. The classic Kantian distinction between active and passive citizens implies that only those citizens who in one way or another actively participate in decision-making are indeed different from the subjects of a non-democratic polity (Weinrib 2008). Participation presumably also has a positive feedback into cognitive awareness of politics as citizens learn about politics while doing it.

Students may have high levels of political interest, enthusiastically follow the news and discuss politics and in the process gain knowledge about politics and form the kinds of opinions about democracy and how it works in their country; however, how does this cognitive engagement with politics translate into political action? Does the fact that students are 'seated closer to the political stage' cognitively, correlate with a more likely active participation and leadership in politics?

This section investigates therefore whether students engage in formal democratic procedures such as voting when they have the opportunity to, involve themselves in various other aspects of active citizenship including membership and leadership of organisations of civil society, participate in meetings and contact officials as well as other forms of informal political participation (such as marching in demonstrations).

5.2.1 Students' participation in elections and identifying with parties

The survey shows that two-thirds of the surveyed students say they voted in the last general election; half of them also voted in the last student election on their campus. Self-reported student turnout to national elections was highest in Kenya, where 79% say they participated in the disputed 2007 election (and one student was 'too young to vote'). Regarding the presidential and parliamentary elections in Tanzania at the end of 2005, 62% of the UDSM students say they have participated (and 19 students said they were still too young then). At UCT; 62% of the students also report to have participated in the last election (which was for most surveyed students the April 2009 election); 39 students say they were 'too young to vote'. In all cases, the number of students who say they 'could not find a polling station' or were 'prevented from voting' is negligible (Figure 34). At the same time, only 31% of students say they feel close to any particular political party (N valid=1 162).

---

19 Further analysis might show that the use of newspapers in particular has an impact on cognitive awareness (as argued by Mattes & Mughogho 2009).

Figure 34 Voter turnout at last national election in comparative perspective

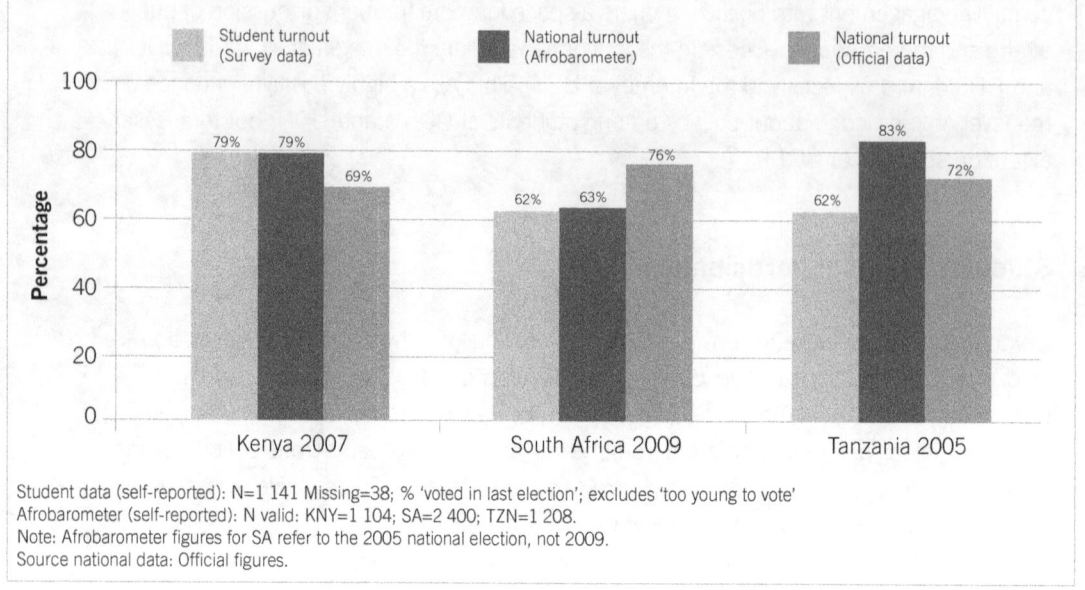

Student data (self-reported): N=1 141 Missing=38; % 'voted in last election'; excludes 'too young to vote'
Afrobarometer (self-reported): N valid: KNY=1 104; SA=2 400; TZN=1 208.
Note: Afrobarometer figures for SA refer to the 2005 national election, not 2009.
Source national data: Official figures.

Turning to the last student elections on campus, here UCT students top the list with 67% indicating that they participated in the 2008/2009 SRC election (even though only 30% correctly name the SRC president who emerged from that election). At UON, 59% of students voted in the 2008/2009 SONU election (and 82% know the Union president), while at UDSM only 25% of the students say they participated in the DARUSO presidential election held in late 2008 (but 62% know the name of the DARUSO president who was elected then) (N valid=1 194).

On the one hand there are clearly anomalies in the data regarding voting behaviour and knowing incumbents. (For instance, how come so many UCT students participate in student elections but then fail to be interested in their outcome?) On the other hand, the relative lesser interest in student elections also correlates with the lack of identification with the student representative structures on all campuses. Less than 20% of students say they feel close to their student representative body (whereby identification is highest with DARUSO at UDSM at 38%, followed by identification with SONU at UON by 15% of students, and least with the UCT SRC at only 6% of students).

5.2.2 Civic participation: meetings, protests

In accordance with the design of the Afrobarometer, the Student Governance Surveys measure a range of ways in which students can participate in politics on and off campus. They include: participating in political meetings; attending demonstrations; personally contacting officials; writing to a newspaper; getting involved in an organisation; or even running for and taking up a formal student leadership position at university.

Table 33 Students' civic participation

		University		
		Nairobi	Cape Town	Dar es Salaam
Collective political action	Attended a political meeting on campus	58%	37%	61%
	Attended a national political meeting	57%	33%	59%
	Attended a student protest/demonstration	29%	21%	50%
	Attended a national protest/demonstration	28%	17%	36%
Individual political action	Wrote a letter to a student paper/pamphlet	9%	7%	9%
	Wrote a letter to a local/national newspaper	21%	6%	14%
	Contacted a senior university official	17%	8%	18%
	Contacted a senior government official	28%	7%	17%

Question: Have you been involved in any of the following activities in the past year?
N valid campus meeting =1 179; N valid national meeting=1 159; N valid student protest=1 168; N valid national protest=1 163; N valid student paper=1 175; N valid national newspaper=1 155; N valid university official=1 178; N valid government official=1 157.

As illustrated in Table 33, there are considerable sections of the student population from each of the three universities that actively participate in politics on and off campus. The majority of respondents from UON and UDSM indicate that they had participated in the last twelve months in political meetings both on and off campus. Over a quarter of respondents at UON and half of UDSM students also attended a national protest once or more often during the last year. In contrast, student participation in political meetings is considerably lower among UCT students (involving only about a third of the student population) and only around a fifth of students from UCT (21%) participated in a student protest and even less (17%) in an off-campus demonstration. However, if one adds the campus-based activism to activism off-campus, UCT students are still considerably more involved in politics than the national average indicates.

Figure 35 Students' participation in national demonstrations

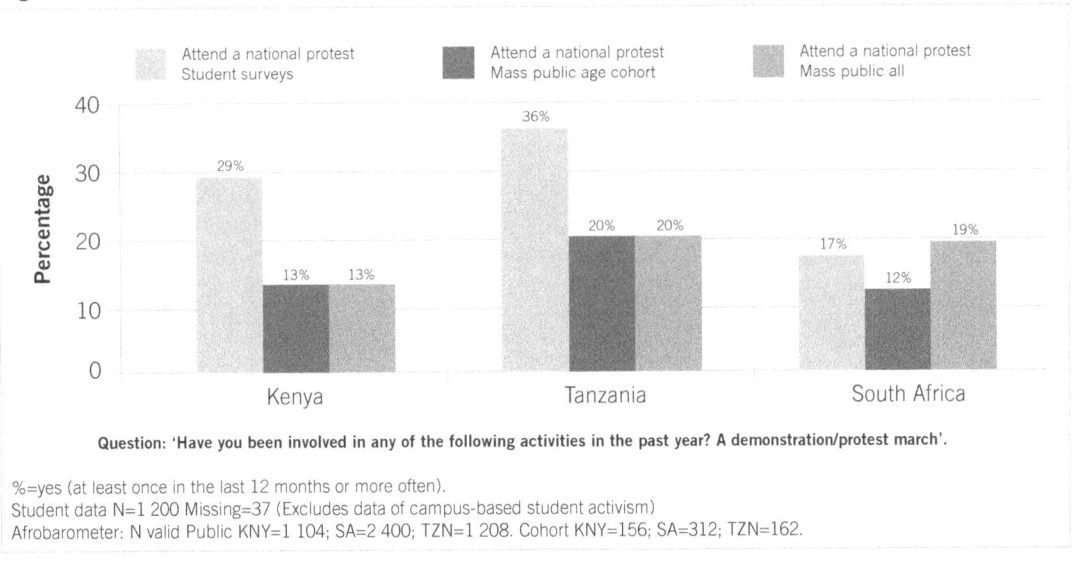

Question: 'Have you been involved in any of the following activities in the past year? A demonstration/protest march'.
%=yes (at least once in the last 12 months or more often).
Student data N=1 200 Missing=37 (Excludes data of campus-based student activism)
Afrobarometer: N valid Public KNY=1 104; SA=2 400; TZN=1 208. Cohort KNY=156; SA=312; TZN=162.

Figure 35 illustrates the finding that students participate much more (UDSM, UON) or to the same degree (UCT) as their fellow citizens in protests and demonstrations that are held off-campus. In particular, whereas only 20% of Tanzanians report that they attended a demonstration or protest in 2008, the figures for students at the University of Dar es Salaam is almost double that (36% for students participating in national protests). Moreover, half of UDSM students report to have been part of a campus-based protest (not displayed). Similarly, while the Afrobarometer reports that 13% of Kenyans participated in demonstrations in 2008, more than double that percentage is true for the Nairobi students (28% for national protests; in addition to 29% for student protests). Lastly, as mentioned already, UCT students are about on par with the national average of 19% for demonstration attendance (17% for national protests; 24% for student protests). The variations between the East African universities is replicated in the variations between these two countries and can therefore be understood in terms of the national political contexts; the South African (UCT) figures, however, follow the trend of earlier findings regarding student engagement at UCT.

While a considerable proportion of students indicate their participation in *collective political activities* such as political meetings and demonstrations, the share of the student body that engages in more *individual political action* is significantly smaller (for data see Table 33 above). Only at the University of Nairobi is the proportion of students who have in the past year written to a newspaper or contacted an official over 20%. At UDSM, under half the number of students who participated in collective political activities ever contacted a senior university or government official to raise a complaint; and even fewer have ever written a letter to an on-campus or off-campus newspaper. The share of individually activist students at UCT is even lower, with less than 10% indicating that they have engaged in any such political activity in the past year. Low levels of contacting formal political leaders and officials have also been observed in the Afrobarometer surveys (with only a 13% African average for contacting government officials) (Gyimah-Boadi & Armah Attoh 2009).

5.2.3 Active organisational memberships and leadership

By means of active membership or leadership of a voluntary organisation either on or off campus, students can participate politically in civil society and thereby claim a place in the public realm as active citizens. Table 34 shows that student participation in associational life is highest in campus-based student organisations. Almost two-thirds of the respondents from all three universities indicate that they are active members or leaders of a non-political student organisation (be it secular or religious). Student involvement in associational life beyond campus is also high – overall 53% of students are members of off-campus groups. Between a third (UCT) and two-thirds (UDSM) of students indicate that they are actively involved in an off-campus secular or religious association.

In comparative perspective it emerges clearly that active membership in voluntary associations is much higher among students than the mass publics. This is especially true for on-campus organisational membership; but even in off-campus secular organisations students are more likely to be active members than both their age cohort without higher education and mass publics. Looking only at student membership in off-campus secular institutions, it can be seen that UDSM students (53%) lead in comparison and that the student figure is considerably higher than the national figure reported by the Afrobarometer.

Equally much higher than the national figure of 16% for South Africa at large (or 11% for the age cohort) is the UCT figure of active off-campus membership of students in non-religious organisations (43%). In Kenya, where the national average is at a high of 43%, active involvement of UON students still beats that with 48% for student membership in off-campus associations (in addition to 63% in on-campus organisations). Student life clearly offers opportunities for organisational involvement both on and off campus which non-students do not have (Figure 36).

Table 34 Civic participation of students: associational memberships

	University		
	Nairobi	Cape Town	Dar es Salaam
Political party	11%	2%	12%
Student union	12%	4%	29%
Non-political student association (secular or religious)	63%	57%	71%
Religious group (off campus)	53%	36%	70%
Voluntary association or club (non-religious) (off-campus)	48%	43%	53%

Question: 'Are you personally involved in any of the following? In what capacity?' %= active member/official leader. N valid political party=1 132; student union =1 130; non-political student association =1 164; religious group (off-campus)=1 151; voluntary association or club (non-religious) (off campus)=1 141

Looking at the active involvement of students in *religious* off-campus groups, a more varied picture emerges (see Figure 37). Students at UDSM are the most actively involved, whereby over 70% indicate active membership or even leadership of an off-campus religious group. This mirrors their high levels of religiosity as well as the high level of involvement in religious groups reported for Tanzanians in general (71% nation-wide).

The South African figures of 39% active involvement pares with the 36% of students at UCT who indicate active membership in off-campus religious groups (while religiosity at UCT is also lower than on the other campuses with 73%) (compare Figure 37).

Lastly, at UON only 53% of the students surveyed report that they are active members of off-campus religious groups while religiosity is indicated at a high 94%. UON students are thus less involved as members in religious organisations than Kenyans overall, of which 66% indicate active membership.

The student surveys therefore show that students tend to be much more actively involved in organisational life in general, including active membership in secular off-campus groups in addition to high levels of campus-based organisational activity. Table 34 (above) also shows that some students take their interest in politics even a step further and become active members of a political party. The relative proportions are higher in East Africa with 11% of UON students and 12% of UDSM students indicating active political party involvement, than at UCT where only 2% of students report party membership.

Figure 36 Student membership in comparative perspective

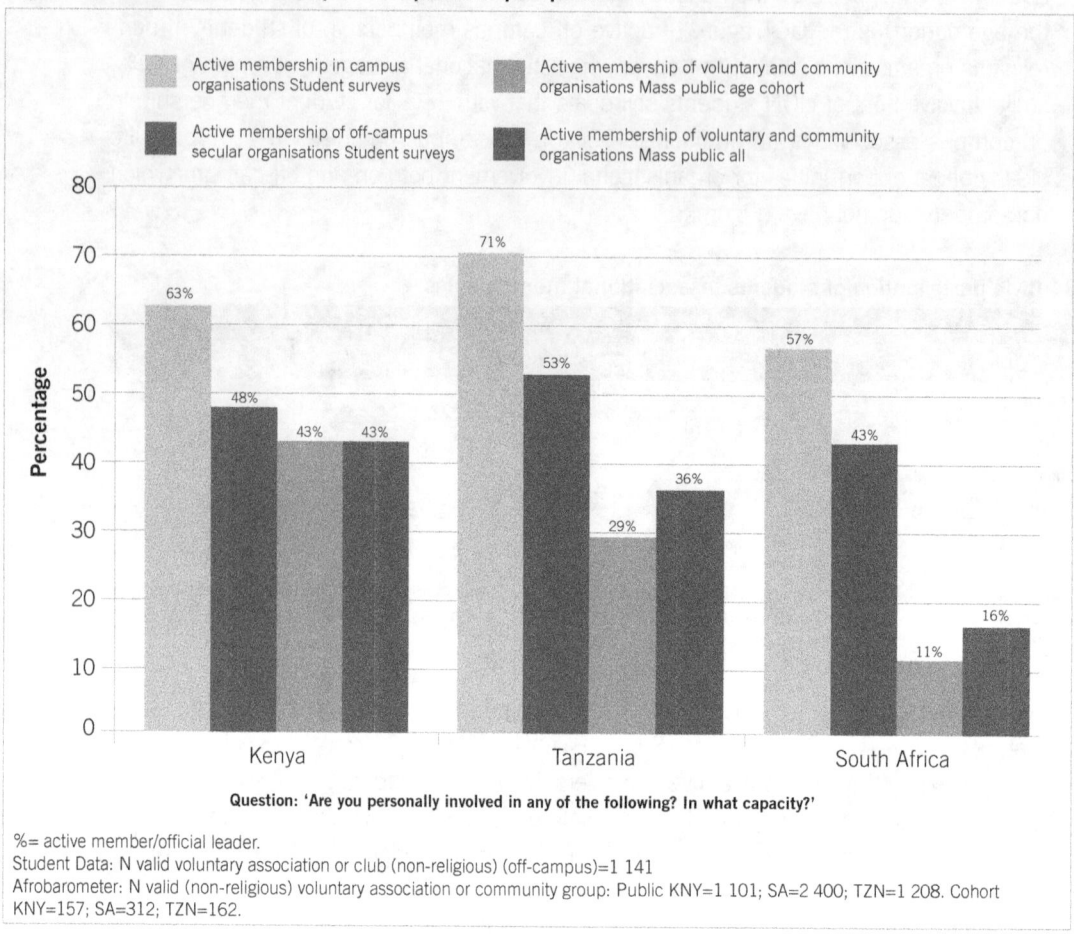

Question: 'Are you personally involved in any of the following? In what capacity?'

%= active member/official leader.
Student Data: N valid voluntary association or club (non-religious) (off-campus)=1 141
Afrobarometer: N valid (non-religious) voluntary association or community group: Public KNY=1 101; SA=2 400; TZN=1 208. Cohort KNY=157; SA=312; TZN=162.

Figure 37 Student membership in religious groups in comparative perspective

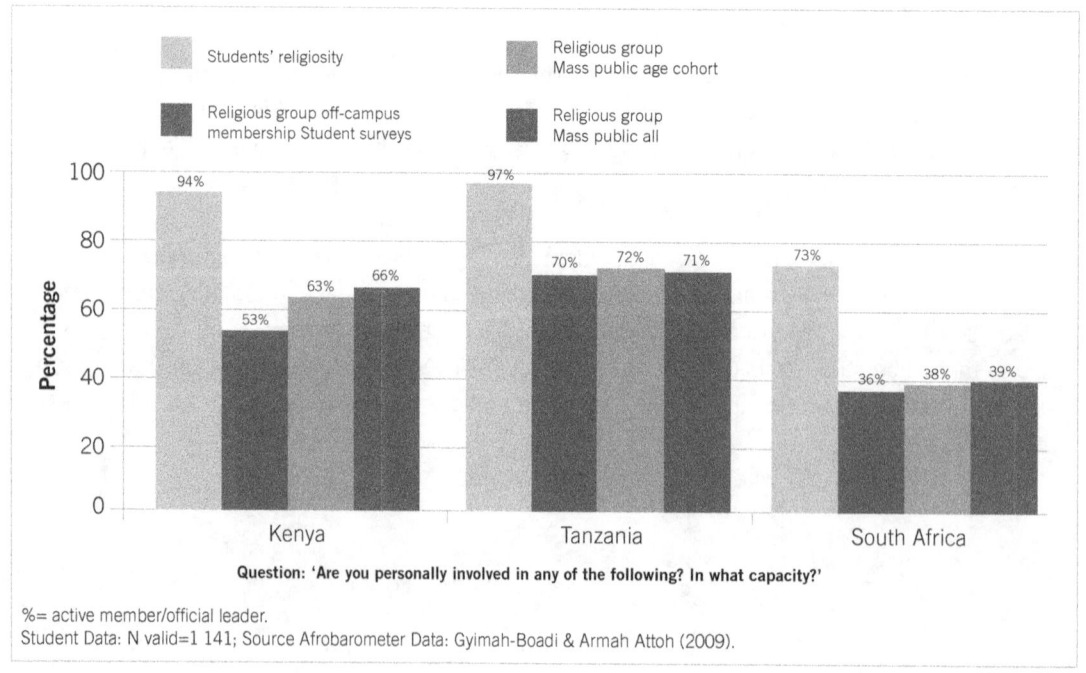

Question: 'Are you personally involved in any of the following? In what capacity?'

%= active member/official leader.
Student Data: N valid=1 141; Source Afrobarometer Data: Gyimah-Boadi & Armah Attoh (2009).

Figure 38 Student leadership of voluntary associations in comparative perspective

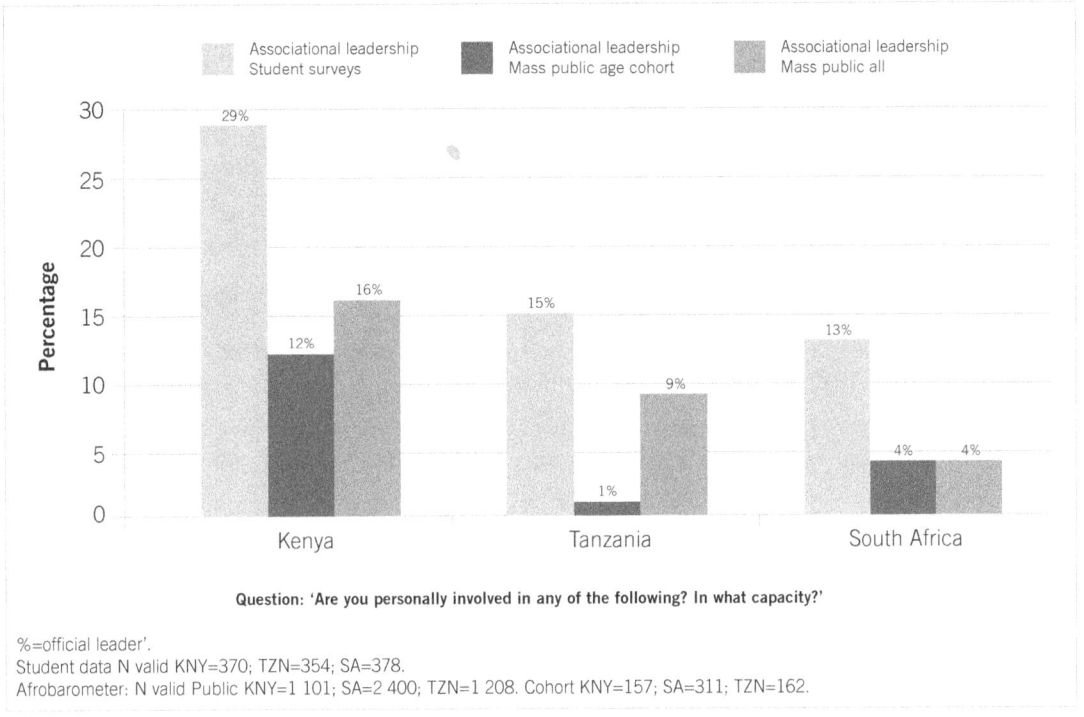

Question: 'Are you personally involved in any of the following? In what capacity?'

%='official leader'.
Student data N valid KNY=370; TZN=354; SA=378.
Afrobarometer: N valid Public KNY=1 101; SA=2 400; TZN=1 208. Cohort KNY=157; SA=311; TZN=162.

Among the advantages that students have in civic life over their age cohort and the mass publics in their country is not only that they are more frequently active members in (especially secular) organisations off-campus over and above a range of campus-based organisations; students are also more likely to be *leaders* of these organisations. Figure 38 shows that between 13% and 29% of students are official leaders of a voluntary, religious or secular association on or off campus. The biggest part of the gap between students and non-students is, as with active membership observed above, the additional opportunity students have by being able to take leadership positions on campus. In other words, the campus-based (non-political) student organisations represent a major potential training ground for the future leadership of civil society in these countries.[20]

Associational life on campus and leadership in campus-based organisations is often considered an important training ground for the new leadership of civil society. This section has shown that there is potential for it to play such a role. The following section therefore looks at the extent to which various forms of student leadership and activism on campus correlate with off-campus political involvement.

5.3 Students as active citizens?

This chapter has shown that being a student at any of the three universities offers clear advantages to the politically interested. Overall, students have better access to a diversity

---

[20] Provided that leaders of campus-based political organisations, and especially student representatives, were oversampled and reweighed at 10% of the total population, leadership of political organisations on campus has been excluded from the analysis in this section. The next section deals with the student political leadership in more detail.

of information about politics, in that politics is much more frequently discussed on campus than among citizens in general and students have more access to and use of a diversity of news media, of which frequent access to the internet as a source of news is almost exclusively a student privilege in Kenya, South Africa and Tanzania.

In addition to the enhanced opportunity for cognitive engagement and media, the university also offers opportunities to pursue political and non-political collective activity for honing civic and leadership skills. Thus, students participate *at least as likely* in national elections, voluntary associations in the community, political meetings and national demonstrations as citizens in general (or even significantly more likely in the cases of UON and UDSM students). In addition, students have a whole palette of campus-based political activities and political and non-political organisations in which to participate and hone their civic and leadership skills, which are not open to the public in general. Thus, looking only at membership of voluntary associations off-campus, UON students are equally as likely, UDSM students double and UCT students three times more likely to be active members than their age peers without higher education. Moreover, students are far more likely to be among the official leadership of these associations than non-students. Over and above that, a majority of students on all campuses are also active members of campus-based voluntary organisations in which many take leadership positions. The Student Governance Surveys therefore provide ample evidence of both cognitive and positional politically relevant advantages offered to students by the university.

This section takes the consideration of students' active citizenship, which is implicit in the analysis of students' cognitive awareness of and participation in politics, a step further and investigates the extent to which student leadership and student activism may serve as a training ground for active citizenship in their country.

5.3.1 Student leadership, activism and active citizenship

In chapter 1, the development of active citizens has been noted as one of the purposes of higher education in democracies. Active citizens participate in public affairs by various means. While a level of cognitive engagement is necessary, active citizenship further involves voting in elections and other forms of citizenship participation. The Student Governance Surveys conceptualised different participatory orientations of students in terms of (1) formal involvement in student leadership; (2) student activism, that is, political involvement outside of formal channels (e.g. protesting); and (3) non-involvement/passive orientation.

As Saha (2000: 13) points out, 'what might be considered legitimate active citizenship in one context, may be considered civil disobedience or even criminal disobedience in another.' This point is not only relevant to keep in mind with respect to the different national contexts in which the surveys were conducted, it also applies to the different levels or spheres where students participate in politics. On the one hand, the distinction between conventional and unconventional political behaviour on campus is somewhat implicit in the distinction between the 'formal student leadership' (made up of elected or appointed official student representatives), and the group of 'student activists' who are defined here as students who have attended one or more demonstrations or protest marches in the past year. On the other hand, whether marching and demonstrating is considered legitimate intra- or extramural citizenship behaviour depends on the local context. Along with investigating these different dimensions of active citizenship, this section also tests the proposition of a student leadership pathway to active citizenship. Is political behaviour at campus level replicated off-campus?

5.3.2 Active citizenship by university

The group of students considered as 'active citizens' refers to those respondents who *always prefer democracy* and have either *participated in a protest on or off campus* in the previous 12 months or *are current/previous student representatives* (SL). If the former group of protesting democrats represents the more unconventionally activist, democratic students, the latter then represents active citizens that prefer formal channels of participation. There is, of course, a considerable overlap between the two types of active citizens whereby 40% of SL can also be considered democratic, protesting active citizens. Overall two-thirds of SL (65%) are active citizens by this definition.

Figure 39 Active citizens: protesting or formally involved democrats

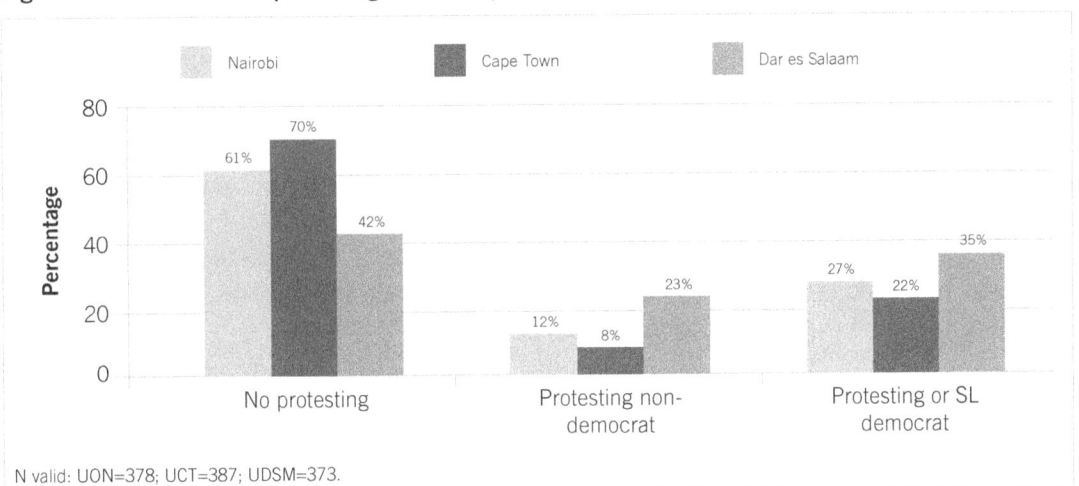

N valid: UON=378; UCT=387; UDSM=373.

Figure 39 shows that the active citizens at the Universities of Cape Town, Dar es Salaam and Nairobi make up only a fraction of the student body: 35% at UDSM, 27% at UON and 22% at UCT. On each campus there is still a smaller group of students who participate in student demonstrations and national demonstrations but who are not always democratically inclined. Furthermore, both at UCT and UON, the majority of students are not participating in protests or demonstrations, whether on or off campus.

5.3.3 Active citizenship in national comparative perspective

In national comparative perspective, the students turn out to be much more likely activist citizens within their respective contexts than their respective age cohort not in higher education and their fellow citizens in general. While students do not necessarily prefer democracy more than the mass publics, the big difference is that those who do so are much more likely to protest or take leadership positions in organisations of civil society and/or student organisations. Thus, among the mass publics, less than a quarter of respondents (in SA even less than a sixth) can be called activist democratic citizens in that they prefer democracy to any other form of government *and* have either attended a protest in the last twelve months or hold an official leadership position in a secular or religious group (or both). Figure 40 illustrates the differences between students and the mass publics.

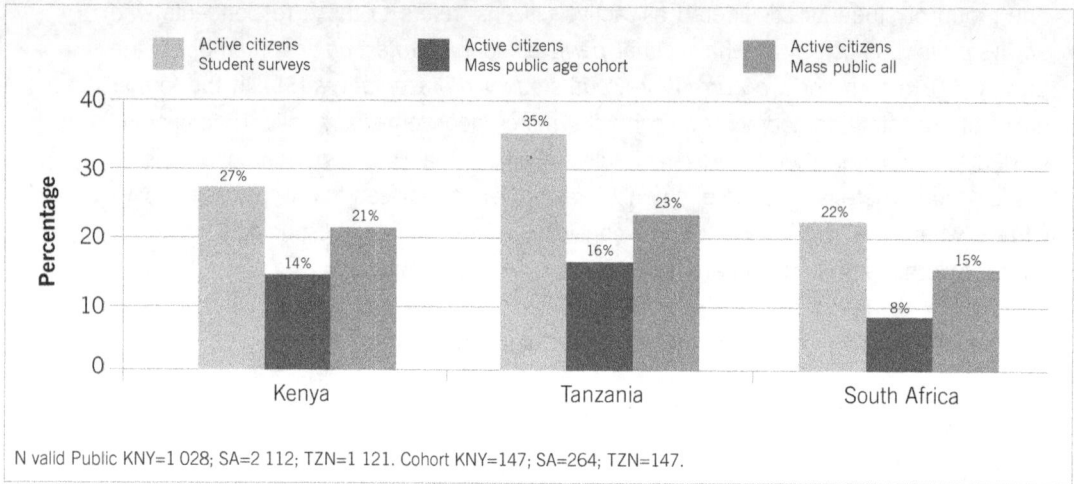

Figure 40 Active citizenship in comparative perspective

While the differences between students and non-students are interesting and noteworthy, the difference between the general public and the youth cohorts without higher education in each country are at least equally interesting, showing that it is *not youthfulness* in general, but tendencies associated with being in higher education, that are likely to account for the more activist disposition of students.

5.3.4 Student political leadership as a training ground?

Participation and leadership in formal settings such as student government on campus and voluntary associations on or off campus are among the typical indicators of active citizenship (Saha 2000: 12). When it comes to leadership in associational life, there are correlations of varying strength between participation in formal student leadership and leadership of voluntary organisations both on and off campus.

Table 35 indicates the extent to which students in formal positions of student government also take leadership in civil society. Strong to moderate correlations exist among formal student leadership and leadership of non-political student organisations at UON and UDSM, and moderate to weak correlations between formal student leadership and leadership in off-campus secular voluntary organisations at UDSM, UON and UCT. When looking at the concrete data it can be seen that at the University of Nairobi, 43% of all formal student leaders are also official leaders of a non-political student organisation (as against 18% of other students; N valid=389); at UCT 26% of formal student leaders also lead a non-political student organisation (as against as against 8% of students not in formal leadership; N valid=395); and at UDSM there are 28% of formal student leaders as against 8% of students not in student government who lead a non-political student organisation (N valid=380). Albeit with less frequency, a similar tendency can also be observed with regard to student leadership in off-campus non-religious organisations (e.g. at UON, 25% of formal student leaders are also leaders of off-campus organisations, as against 9% of other students; N valid=383).

These correlations suggest that students in formal leadership roles on campus have a tendency to also take leadership in non-political on- and off-campus associations. In this respect, formal student representation on campus could serve as a training ground for leadership in civil society as the skills and competencies acquired in the university context could immediately be transferred to organised civil society beyond campus (and vice versa).

Table 35 Student leaders taking leadership in civil society

	University		
	Nairobi	Cape Town	Dar es Salaam
Formal student leader / Leader of a non-political student organisation	Pearson .432** Sig. (2-tailed) .000 N valid 375	n/s	Pearson .667** Sig. (2-tailed) .000 N valid 359
Formal student leader / Leader in a non-religious association off campus	Pearson .155** Sig. (2-tailed) .002 N valid 383	Pearson .142** Sig. (2-tailed) .005 N valid 385	Pearson .432** Sig. (2-tailed) .000 N valid 375
Leader in a non-religious association off campus / Leader in a religious group off campus	Pearson .269** Sig. (2-tailed) .000 N valid 379	Pearson .153** Sig. (2-tailed) .003 N valid 382	n/s

** Correlation is significant at the 0.01 level (2-tailed). Control variables: involvement/non-involvement on/off campus in religious/non-religious organisations. Only the strongest correlations are displayed.

Moreover, involvement in formal student leadership on campus is also correlated with participation in student activism and other forms of civic participation. Among students at the University of Nairobi, there are moderate to weak correlations between formal student leadership and involvement in political activism. Weak correlations in this regard can also be found in the UCT and UDSM data.

Table 36 indicates significant moderate to weak correlations between being a student representative and participating in various forms of political activism (attending political meetings, protests, contacting officials, and writing letters to newspapers) on and off campus. Among students of the University of Nairobi, there are moderate to weak correlations between formal student leadership and involvement in political activism. Weak correlations in this regard can also be found in the UCT and UDSM data.

By far the strongest significant correlations in this investigation are found between those who behave as political activists on campus as well as off campus. There appears to be a significant group of students who are *not* in formal student leadership positions but who participate extensively in political activism on and off campus. In this respect Table 36 shows that at all three universities, there is a fairly strong correlation between those

Table 36 Student leaders and political activism

	University					
	Nairobi		Cape Town		Dar es Salaam	
Formal student leader / Index of campus-level political activism	Pearson Sig. (2-tailed) N valid	**.397** .000 397	Pearson Sig. (2-tailed) N valid	**.168** .001 399	Pearson Sig. (2-tailed) N valid	**.233** .000 397
Formal student leader / Index of national-level political activism	Pearson Sig. (2-tailed) N valid	**.240** .000 385	Pearson Sig. (2-tailed) N valid	**.134** .008 391	Pearson Sig. (2-tailed) N valid	**.198** .000 391
Index of campus-level / Index of national level political activism	Pearson Sig. (2-tailed) N valid	**.614** .000 385	Pearson Sig. (2-tailed) N valid	**.781** .000 390	Pearson Sig. (2-tailed) N valid	**.565** .000 389
Attend political meeting on campus / off campus	Pearson Sig. (2-tailed) N valid	**.420** .000 378	Pearson Sig. (2-tailed) N valid	**.640** .000 390	Pearson Sig. (2-tailed) N valid	**.400** .000 378
Attend protest or demonstration on campus / off campus	Pearson Sig. (2-tailed) N valid	**.604** .000 379	Pearson Sig. (2-tailed) N valid	**.619** .000 386	Pearson Sig. (2-tailed) N valid	**.478** .000 373

** Correlation is significant at the 0.01 level (2-tailed). Control variables: all civil participation variables on/off-campus. Only the strongest correlations are displayed.

students who participate in student political activism on campus and those who do so off campus (UCT .781**; UON .614**; UDSM .565**). This correlation also holds (albeit not as strongly) when identifying specific political activities such as attending political meetings or protest marches.

5.3.5 Student politics and political specialisation

A way of understanding these findings is to consider student political leadership as a series of related activities for which politically-inclined students specialise. In this regard, leadership within a formal organisational context can be considered a type of student political specialisation, whereby leaders in student government also tend to act as leaders in other formal organisational contexts such as non-political student organisations and off-campus voluntary associations (compare Table 35).

A second type of specialisation is evident from Table 36. Moderate to strong correlations are evident between the indices of on-campus and off-campus political activism (especially with regard to attending political meetings and participating in protests). This suggests that student participation in informal collective political activity is a second type of student political specialisation. The table indicates clearly that the correlation between student participation in collective campus-level political activism and corresponding off-campus political activities is strong and robust across all three universities.

5.4 Summary and conclusion

This chapter has considered students' cognitive engagement with politics and political participation in different forms on and off campus. It has shown that students are not necessarily more interested in politics than citizens in general; however, students have a cognitive advantage over the public in general in that politics is discussed more frequently on campus and students have frequent access to a diversity of news media, of which access to the internet in particular is almost exclusive to students in Kenya, South Africa and Tanzania. Whether the advantages for cognitive engagement provided by the university environment translate into better knowledge about politics cannot be said conclusively. It is clear, however, that all three universities provide a privileged place for cognitive engagement with politics.

The same can also be said with respect to political participation. Especially the University of Dar es Salaam and the University of Nairobi appear to provide havens for political activity with high levels of student involvement in political meetings and demonstrations on campus. Yet even at UCT students are more likely to participate in protests than mass publics when one adds their on and off campus experiences. In comparative perspective it also emerges that students' active membership of voluntary associations is much higher than that of mass publics. Not only is it higher in off-campus organisations, it is further augmented by participation in various on-campus student organisations. Moreover, leadership of voluntary associations (off-campus) is far more likely among students than non-students. In other words, university and student life present unmatched opportunities for exercising political activity and organisational leadership at a young age. Students therefore are not only seated closer to the political action as observers but also as political actors.

While students in general thus emerge among the most active citizens in their respective countries, the chapter finds that formal student leadership only weakly (or moderately in the UON case) correlates with informal political activity on campus, and weakly (in all three universities) with informal political activity off-campus. Rather, formal student leadership (i.e. student representation in university governance structures) and leadership in other formal organisational contexts, on the one hand; and informal collective political activity on and off campus on the other hand; represent somewhat distinct political specialisations for students on all three campuses. Thus, the university potentially offers a training ground for active citizenship in formally organised civil society as well as in informal and more unconventional forms of political participation.

Chapter 6
Student Politics and the University: Implications and Recommendations

6.1 Overview of the findings

Overall the Student Governance Surveys have shown that students understand what democracy is, and that they understand democracy mostly in procedural terms. Their definitions of democracy have mostly positive connotations. Over two-thirds of students support democracy; and around half of the students are exclusively committed to democracy (more at UCT and less at UDSM). The survey shows that commitment to democracy, as measured in terms of preference for democracy and rejection of non-democratic alternatives, neither increases nor decreases significantly with involvement in student governance or other forms of student political participation.

Students' perception of the extent to which their national political system can be called a democracy is consistently *far more critical* than that of mass publics (especially among the East African students). Students at UON are least satisfied with the way their government works (87% 'not satisfied') while UCT students are most satisfied (57% 'fairly'/'very satisfied').

Taking the notions of equilibrium/disequilibrium between demand for democracy and supply of democracy as indicators for the extent to which an existing regime is considered consolidated as a democracy, it emerges that the Kenyan political system is a fairly liberal but *unconsolidated* regime, ready for pro-democratic regime change from a student perspective (which, referring to the coalition government of 2009, is a perceptive assessment). The same analysis suggests that the Tanzanian political system is also a fairly liberal political system that is not fully consolidated and offers room for reform and deepening of democracy from a student perspective (but less so from the perspective of Tanzanians in general), and that South Africa's liberal democracy is fairly consolidated from the UCT students' perspective. Correspondingly, a majority of UON students emerge as the most critical and impatient democrats (in national and cross-campus comparison), while the number of complacent and fairly uncritical democrats is highest among UCT students. The comparison with Afrobarometer data shows that the students from all three campuses are significantly more likely to be critical and impatient, transformative democrats than their respective fellow citizens and their same age peers without higher education.

The surveys further show that all the three universities provide access to a greater diversity of news media than what is available to mass publics. Universities provide better access to newspapers and TV (in Kenya and Tanzania), and students at all three university/country contexts have *almost exclusively* access to frequent use of the internet. In addition, students tend to discuss politics more frequently than mass publics. Thus, students emerge as well informed about politics (at UON/UDSM better than mass publics, at UCT slightly worse). And yet, while students discuss politics *more frequently* than mass publics and are more frequently using a diversity of news media, they are actually *not more interested* in public affairs than the public in general. With respect to cognitive engagement, all three universities may therefore be considered akin to a *hothouse* in that they provide a unique environment for awareness and knowledge about politics to blossom. However, once a student leaves the university the hothouse effect may well disappear.

The universities also provide ample opportunity for students to participate in political activity and to take leadership in voluntary associations on and off campus. The surveys show that students specialise in certain types of political participation at university. Thus, while those in formal student leadership positions tend to also take up official leadership positions in off-campus voluntary associations, student activists are also typically activists (e.g. protesters) engaged in civil society beyond campus. The analysis of the student surveys and Afrobarometer data in terms of the notion of 'active citizenship' shows that relatively higher levels of active political participation of students is not an effect of their youthfulness but more likely the effect of specific predispositions and conditions associated with being at university. Thus, these findings suggest that the university has the potential to be a *training ground* in democracy for the upcoming leadership of state and civil society.

6.2 Enhancing the university's training ground potential

In order to enhance and actualise the university's potential to act as a training ground for democratic citizenship, several findings of the surveys related to students' political participation have to be taken into account: Students mostly participate in collective political activity; the strongest correlations in the survey have been found between students' participation in politics on campus and off campus; the types of political participation engaged in on campus and off campus are often the same ... and so forth. While the first finding is typical for political participation in Africa overall, the latter two point towards a possibility of a student pathway to leadership in civil society. The potential of the university as a site of citizenship development is further enhanced when one looks at various other correlations of students' attitudes towards politics and political behaviour on and off campus (e.g. with respect to perceptions of leadership corruption and trust).

Confronted with student activism, the tendency of university administrations in Africa is typically to either respond with utmost severity to the student challenge, for example by calling in the police, criminalising student leaders, collectively punishing students with university closure, the banning of student organisations and the destruction of student businesses and so forth.[21] Alternatively, the strategy has also been to incorporate (or outrightly co-opt) the student leadership in more or less effective ways into the formal machinery of university decision-making (or a combination of the two). In most cases, the objective of the university's response is to *discourage* and *de-emphasise* mass participation of students in political activity and to *sanitize* student leaders' involvement in politics on and off campus. This is done in the name of restoring and maintaining a peaceful academic environment conducive to learning.

However, an academic environment where a sprinkling of students is co-opted into enjoying the spoils of office, while the majority of students are politically de-activated only to be 'mobilised' occasionally as 'masses' by student leaders for their own purposes (of name, fame and often financial gain) is not one conducive to students' learning how to take up the rights and responsibilities of democratic citizenship, or one in which students can learn how to exert democratic leadership in civil society.

Rather, the Student Governance Surveys suggest that to depoliticise the university and sanitize student politics is to lose out on the very vehicle which African universities can use to make a key contribution to the democratisation of political culture. The study suggests that it is precisely by enhancing student involvement in collective political and non-political activity and supporting student leadership in a variety of organisational contexts, that the university can make a contribution to democratic citizenship.

6.2.1 Students' preferences for university governance

The majority of students at the Universities of Cape Town, Dar es Salaam and Nairobi look to the university to provide them with the kind of qualification that will enable them to find quality employment in the market place and to provide them with an education of the highest international standard (N valid UCT 376, UON 342, UDSM 347). Students see the university first and foremost as an academic facility and a community of learning; moreover a sizeable group also concedes to a national developmental mandate for the university (most at UDSM, least at UCT). The conception of the university as a service provider and private business finds, however, almost no support among students of all three student bodies.

Corresponding to these conceptions of the university, students agree with specific ways that the university should be governed. Overall, students prefer the university to be governed in a manner that is inclusive of all key constituencies. Decisions about the university should be made predominantly by internal constituencies (especially senior management, the professoriate, and students) in keeping with their respective criteria and interests.

Students have a rather idealistic view of the possible extent of student participation in university governance. On the one hand, students demand to be involved in making key decisions in the university along with institutional management and academics. Over 80%

---

[21] This precise scenario has been recounted to the researchers by officers in the office of the dean of students and student leaders as the 2008 university response to a series of student protests at one of the three surveyed universities.

Figure 41 Students' conceptions of the university

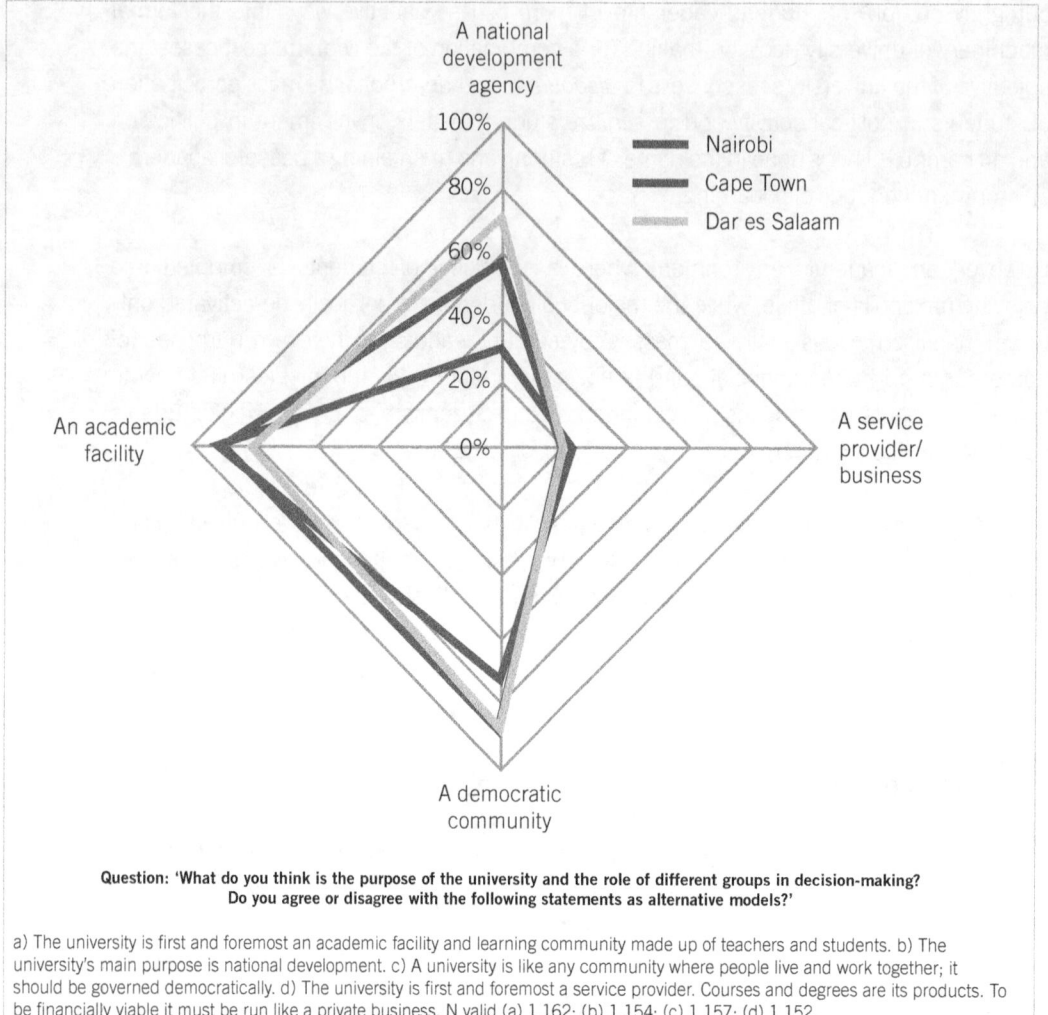

Question: 'What do you think is the purpose of the university and the role of different groups in decision-making? Do you agree or disagree with the following statements as alternative models?'

a) The university is first and foremost an academic facility and learning community made up of teachers and students. b) The university's main purpose is national development. c) A university is like any community where people live and work together; it should be governed democratically. d) The university is first and foremost a service provider. Courses and degrees are its products. To be financially viable it must be run like a private business. N valid (a) 1 162; (b) 1 154; (c) 1 157; (d) 1 152.

of students on all campuses disagree with the notion that student involvement in university decision-making is '*a waste of time from everybody involved*' (N valid 1 180); rather almost as many argue that '*student representation in the University Council, Senate and their committees ensures that the student voice is heard*' (N valid 1 175). Students want to be involved in sensitive areas of university governance such as the appointment of academics and top managers, and they want to have a voice at the highest levels of decision-making, including University Council and Senate. Yet, the idea that '*students [should] have the predominant voice and run the university responsive to student interests*' gains very mixed support on the three campuses. At UON a majority of students would agree (54%); at UDSM 47% of students agree while at UCT only 35% of students support this idea (N valid UON 390, UDSM 390, UCT 396). The proposal of equality among the different internal constituencies (i.e. academics, management, students) receives more support, whereby the sizable majority (UDSM/UON) or close-to-majority (UCT) of students on all three campuses supports '*same rights and powers to participate in university decision-making like other constituencies*' for students ('agree'/'strongly agree' UON: 67% of 378; UCT 48% of 388; UDSM 81% of 395; rest mostly indifferent).

6.2.2 Rethinking student representation and student development

The overwhelming student support for student participation in representative decision-making forums comes in a context where student representation itself faces a crisis of legitimacy. At UON, less than 20% of students are satisfied with the way student representation works in their institution (N valid 396), and only 26% consider the last student election free and fair (N valid 390). The situation is only marginally better at UDSM ('fairly'/'very satisfied' 24% of 400; elections 'free'/'fair with/without minor problems' 27% of 396); while at UCT, just over 50% of students consider student representation adequate or almost adequate (N valid 396).

Moreover, student representatives are among the *least* trusted groups on campus and perceived as more corrupt than management and academics. At UON only 19% of students say they trust student leaders (while over 52% trust their fellow students; N valid 396); conversely, over 70% of students think that most or all of their student leaders are involved in corruption. At UDSM, about half of the students not in leadership trust their student leaders (202 of 395), and about a third think student leadership is involved in corruption (30% of 396). Even at UCT, student leaders are the *least* trusted group (between student leaders, management and academics), albeit levels of trust are much higher there than on the East African campuses. While two-thirds of UCT students trust other students on campus, almost 80% trust senior management and over 90% trust the university's academics and professors; student leaders in turn have only gained the trust of just over half the UCT student population (58%; N valid 399). Furthermore, even at UCT student leaders are more often perceived corrupt than any of the other university constituencies (i.e. top managers and academics) (albeit at a low level with 16% of 397).

In a previous paper we have shown that levels of trust and the perception of the responsiveness of student leaders to students in general are moderately positively correlated with each other, and moderately negatively correlated with perceptions of student leadership corruption (Luescher-Mamashela 2010a). Thus, it may be expected that as student leadership responsiveness increases, levels of trust increase and perceptions of corruption decrease. Correspondingly, perceptions of student leadership corruption may therefore decrease as levels of trust and responsiveness increase. How can levels of trust and responsiveness be increased and simultaneously perceptions (and practices) of corruption be reduced?

6.2.3 Developing citizenship through student development

On the one hand, students' demand for representative, democratic university governance is seemingly thwarted by the way university governance and student representation is perceived to work (especially at UON and UDSM). On the other hand, students' relative lack of trust in student leadership and perception of corruption offers an opportunity to rethink the way student representation works. Looking at the training ground potential of the university, these findings suggest *greater involvement of the university management and academics* in making student representation work for students, rather than less. This does not mean micro-managing student government; rather it suggests that by empowering students and student leaders to make their contribution to the university in more democratic and effective ways, the university can make a significant contribution to citizenship development.

Without wanting to delve into the details of specific training and support programmes that offices of student development and Deans of Students might want to develop, there are various concrete ways by which effective and inexpensive solutions can be implemented.[22] For instance, specific training to emerging student leaders could focus on leadership responsibilities in formal settings, for example developing a mission and purpose for an organisation; democratically choosing leaders; evaluating and supporting leaders; ensuring good management; being accountable for financial resources; developing and implementing a strategic plan; monitoring institutional development and transformation; being responsible for ensuring good order and a safe campus environment and developing and preserving institutional autonomy in a context of responsiveness to developmental needs etc. (Ncayiyana & Hayward 1999).

Developing a consensus on the operational and organisational parameters of student activity and politics should be set in consultation with student leadership along with policies as to the rules by which certain organisations are allowed to operate on campus. At UCT, for instance, political parties were banned from campus for most of the apartheid era but were allowed to establish branches on campus just before the democratic breakthrough in 1994. They now operate under the same rules as any other student organisations and play an important role in formal student leadership. Consideration must be given whether certain off-campus organisations should specifically be encouraged to establish student branches (e.g. Habitat for Humanity; Doctors without Borders) and correspondingly, student organisations who reach out charitably beyond campus might deserve special assistance and support to do so more effectively from student development offices.

Student entrepreneurship, on and off campus, provides opportunity for special support and attention from university management. In many of these respects the university management should act as an honest (and disinterested) broker, ensuring continuity and institutional memory across generations of student leadership along with monitoring to ensure that distributional politics do not become spoils politics. Student sport clubs, recreational, artistic and academic organisations, together with the student union/guild and student governments, offer the organisational context for students to train in various leadership capacities while exercising their talents or special interests. Lastly, support for a regular and high-quality student news medium (e.g. an online and/or print student newspaper) published in a context of responsible free speech and freedom of the press on campus and accessible to all members of the campus community should be a priority.

---

22 At the University of Cape Town, an 'Emerging Student Leaders Programme' has been developed and implemented which annually offers co-curricular training in student leadership by means of seminars and conferences to over 100 competitively selected emerging student leaders.

CHAPTER 6 STUDENT POLITICS AND THE UNIVERSITY: IMPLICATIONS AND RECOMMENDATIONS

In short, the potential of the university acting as a training ground for democratic citizenship can be actualised and enhanced by strengthening student development in various student organisational and leadership contexts through specific training as well as targeted support.

The Student Governance Surveys have shown that university and student life present unmatched opportunities for exercising political activity and organisational leadership at a young age. Students are not only seated closer to the political action as critical observers, they *are* political actors who operate both on and off campus. While the university and various aspects of student life offer a potential training ground for transformative and active citizenship (both in conventional and unconventional forms of political participation), there is an equally likely potential for high levels of citizenship involvement to disappear once certain 'hothouse conditions' (e.g. with respect to cognitive engagement and political participation) are removed upon leaving the university. The potential contribution of specific curricular interventions to support democratic citizenship is not denied, but they have not been the focus of this study. Rather, looking at students' political attitudes and behaviours, and particularly at political participation, there is clearly a potential of the university acting as training ground for an emerging democratic leadership of state and civil society. In this respect, it is apposite to re-emphasise Bleiklie's point that citizenship education involves mode 1 and mode 2 types of knowledge, suggesting that 'students need to learn **how** democracy works' and learn to appreciate '**that** democracy works by experiencing that they can influence events and their own living conditions through participation' (n.d.: 1, *original emphasis*). In both respects, co- and extra-curricular interventions by student development offices provide a way of fostering knowledge about democracy and democratisation. Among the key findings supporting this point are correlations of on- and off-campus student participation in political and civil society activity which suggest a distinct mechanism, a student leadership pathway, to democratic citizenship and leadership of civil society. Thus, strengthening student development in various student organisational and leadership contexts through specific training and targeted support represents a key opportunity for the university to simultaneously enhance student life as well as the university's contribution to democracy. In this respect, by developing students' capacity for democratic leadership on campus, the university fosters democratic leadership in civil society and ultimately democracy in the country.

References

Afrobarometer (2009a) Popular Attitudes towards Democracy in Kenya: A Summary of Afrobarometer Indicators, 2001–2008. Available at: www.afrobarometer.org [accessed 14 July 2010]

Afrobarometer (2009b) Popular Attitudes towards Democracy in South Africa: A Summary of Afrobarometer Indicators, 2001–2008. Available at: www.afrobarometer.org [accessed 14 July 2010]

Afrobarometer (2009c) Popular Attitudes towards Democracy in Tanzania: A Summary of Afrobarometer Indicators, 2001–2008. Available at: www.afrobarometer.org [accessed 14 July 2010]

Afrobarometer (2010) Official Website of the Afrobarometer. Available at: www.afrobarometer.org [accessed 14 July 2010]

Altbach PG (1989) Perspectives on Student Political Activism. In: Altbach PG (ed) *Student Political Activism: An International Reference Handbook*. New York: Greenwood

Altbach PG (1991) Student Political Activism. In: Altbach PG (ed.) *International Higher Education: An Encyclopedia*. New York: Garland Publishing

Altbach PG (2006) Student Politics: Activism and Culture. In: Forest JFJ & Altbach PG (eds) *International Handbook of Higher Education*. Dordrecht: Springer

ARW (2009) Academic Ranking of World Universities. Available at: http://www.arwu.org/ARWU2009.jsp [accessed 8 June 2010]

Badat SM (1999) *Black Student Politics, Higher Education and Apartheid: From SASO to SANSCO, 1968–1990*. Pretoria: Human Sciences Research Council

Bleiklie I (n.d.) Educating for Citizenship. Report submitted to the Working Party 'Universities as sites of citizenship', CC-HER, Council of Europe. Available at: http://www.upenn.edu/ccp/intlconsortium/research/university_sites/monographs/MonographNorway.pdf [accessed 12 December 2010]

Bratton M & Mattes R (2009) Neither Consolidating nor Fully Democratic: The Evolution of African Political Regimes, 1999–2008. *Afrobarometer Briefing Paper* No. 67 (May 2009). Cape Town: CSSR. Available at: www.afrobarometer.org [accessed 14 July 2010]

Bunting I, Sheppard C, Cloete N, & Belding L (2010) *Performance Indicators: South African Higher Education 2000–2008*. Wynberg: CHET

Daun H, Enslin P, Kolouh-Westin L & Plut D (2002) *Democracy in Textbooks and Student Minds: Educational Transitions in Bosnia-Herzegovina, Yugoslavia, Mozambique and South Africa.* New York: Nova Science

Department of Education (1997) *Education White Paper 3: A Programme for Higher Education Transformation (WPHE).* Pretoria: Department of Education

Evans G & Rose P (2007) Support for Democracy in Malawi: Does Schooling Matter? *World Development* 35(5): 904–919

Finkel SE (2002) Civic education and the mobilization of political participation in developing democracies. *The Journal of Politics* 64(4): 994–1020

Frazer E (1998) Book Review: Education and Democratic Citizenship in America. *Journal of Public Policy* 18(1): 101–103

Gyimah-Boadi E & Armah Attoh D (2009) Are Democratic Citizens emerging in Africa? Evidence from the Afrobarometer. *Afrobarometer Briefing Paper.* No. 70 (May 2009). Cape Town: CSSR. Available at: www.afrobarometer.org [accessed 14 July 2010]

Heilman B (2010) *Countries at the Crossroads 2010: Country Report – Tanzania.* Available at: www.freedomhouse.org [accessed 8 June 2010]

Hoskins B, D'Hombres B & Campbell J (2008) Does formal education have an impact on active citizenship behaviour? *European Educational Research Journal* 7(3): 386–402

Huntington SP (1991) *The Third Wave: Democratisation in the Late Twentieth Century.* Norman: University of Oklahoma Press

Hyden G (1992) Governance and the Study of Politics. In: Hyden G & Bratton M (eds) *Governance and Politics in Africa.* Boulder: Lynne Rienner

Ichilov O (1990) Dimensions and role patterns of citizenship and democracy. In: Ichilov O (ed.) *Political Socialization, Citizenship Education and Democracy.* New York and London: Teachers College Press, Columbia University

IIAG (2009) Ibrahim Index of African Governance. Available at: http://www.moibrahimfoundation.org/en/section/the-ibrahim-index [accessed 8 June 2010]

Inglehart R (2003) How solid is mass support for democracy – and how can we measure it? PSOnline. Available at: www.apsanet.org [accessed 20 June 2010]

Ismail Z & Graham P (2009) Citizens of the World? Africans, Media and Telecommunications. *Afrobarometer Briefing Paper* No. 69 (May 2009). Cape Town: CSSR. Available at: www.afrobarometer.org [accessed 14 July 2010]

Klopp JM & Orina JR (2002) University Crisis, Student Activism, and the Contemporary Struggle for Democracy in Kenya *African Studies Review* 45(1): 43–76

Lasner T (2010) *Countries at the Crossroads 2010: Country Report – Kenya.* Available at: www.freedomhouse.org [accessed 8 June 2010]

Luescher TM (2005) *Student Governance in Africa.* Paper presented at the Seminar on Improving Governance and Student Leadership, organised by the Centre for Higher Education Transformation at the University of Stellenbosch, South Africa, 01 April. [Online]. Available at: http://www.chet.org.za [accessed 9 November 2005]

Luescher TM (2009). *Student Governance in Transition: University Democratisation and Managerialism. A Governance Approach to the Study of Student Politics and the Case of the University of Cape Town.* Doctoral dissertation. Cape Town: University of Cape Town

Luescher-Mamashela TM (2010a) *Student Perceptions of Student Leadership in Africa: Involved, Responsive, Corrupt.* Presentation made at the African Student Leaders' Summit, 8 Sept., Cape Town, South Africa. Available online: www.chet.org.za. [accessed 15 November 2010]

Luescher-Mamashela TM (2010b) University Democratisation and Managerialism in South Africa: The Changing Legitimation of University Governance and the Place of Students. *Tertiary Education and Management* 16(4): 259–283.

Maghoa GOA (2008) Speech delivered by Prof. George AO Magoha, Vice-Chancellor, University of Nairobi during the 39th Graduation Ceremony at the Chancellor's Court. 17 October 2008. Available at: http://www.uonbi.ac.ke/administration/speeches/VC_Speech_39Grad.pdf [accessed 23 November 2010]

Maghoa GOA (2009) Speech delivered by Prof. George AO Magoha, Vice-Chancellor, University of Nairobi during the 42nd Graduation Ceremony at the Chancellor's Court. 4 December 2009. Available at: http://www.uonbi.ac.ke/administration/speeches/42ndGraduationVCSpeech.pdf [accessed 23 November 2010]

Mattes R, Davids YD & Africa C (1999) Views of Democracy in South Africa and the Region: Trends and Comparisons. *South African Democracy Barometer.* Cape Town: Idasa

Mattes R & Mughogho D (2010) *The Limited Impacts of Formal Education on Democratic Citizenship in Africa.* HERANA Research Report. Cape Town: CHET. Available at: www.chet.org.za [accessed 8 August 2010]

Mintz E, Close D & Croci O (2006) *Politics, Power and the Common Good: An Introduction to Political Science.* Toronto: Pearson Prentice Hall

Mkude D, Cooksey B & Levey L (2003) *Higher Education in Tanzania: A Case Study.* Dar es Salaam: Mkuki Na Nyota

Muller EN, Seligson MA & Turan I (1987) Education, Participation, and Support for Democratic Norms. *Comparative Politics* 20(1): 19–33

Munck GL & Leff CS (1997) Modes of Transition and Democratization: South America and Eastern Europe in Comparative Perspective. *Comparative Politics* 29(3): 343–362

Munene I (2003) Student Activism in African Higher Education. In: Teferra D & Altbach PG (eds) *African Higher Education: An International Reference Handbook.* Bloomington: Indiana University Press

Mwiria K & Ng'ethe N (2007) Reforms related to Governance/Management & Planning. In: Mwiria K, Ng'ethe N, Ngome C, Ouma-Odero D, Wawire V and Wesonga D (eds) *Public & Private Universities in Kenya: New Challenges, Issues & Achievements.* Oxford: James Currey and Nairobi: East African Educational Publishers.

Mwollo-ntallima A (2011) Higher Education and Democracy: A Study of Students' and Student Leaders' Attitudes towards Democracy in Tanzania. Master's dissertation. University of the Western Cape, Bellville, South Africa

Ncayiyana DJ & Hayward FM (1999) *Effective Governance: A Guide for Council Members of Universities and Technikons.* Pretoria: CHET

Nduko J (2000) Students' Rights and Academic Freedom in Kenya's Public Universities. In: Federici S, Caffentzis G and Alidou O (eds) *A Thousand Flowers: Social Struggles Against Structural Adjustment in African Universities.* Trenton, N.J.: Africa Word Press

Nie NH, Junn J & Stehlik-Barry K (1996) *Education and Democratic Citizenship in America.* Chicago and London: The University of Chicago Press.

Perkin H (2006) History of Universities. In: Forest JFJ and Altbach PG (eds) *International Handbook of Higher Education.* Dordrecht: Springer

Plantan F (2002) *Universities as Sites of Citizenship and Civic Responsibility.* Final General Report – February 2002. Available at: http://www.coe.int [accessed 12 December 2010]

Puddington A (2009). The 2008 Freedom House Survey: A Third Year of Decline. *The Journal of Democracy* 20(2): 93–107

Rosenberg MY (2010) *Countries at the Crossroads 2010: Country Report – South Africa.* Available at: www.freedomhouse.org [accessed 8 June 2010]

Saha LJ (2000) Education and Active Citizenship. *Educational Practice and Theory* 22(1): 9–20

Schmidt MG (1995) *Wörterbuch zur Politik.* Stuttgart: Alfred Kröner Verlag

SONU (2010) *The Constitution of the Students' Organisation of the University of Nairobi (SONU).* Available at: http://www.uonbi.ac.ke/student-life/SONU_2010_CONSTITUTION.pdf [accessed 22 November 2010]

UCT (2010) *Official Website of the University of Cape Town.* Available at: http://www.uct.ac.za [accessed 22 November 2010]

UON (2010). *Official Website of the University of Nairobi.* Available at: http://www.uonbi.ac.ke [accessed 22 November 2010]

Von Lieres B & Robins S (2008) Democracy and citizenship. In: Shepherd N and Robins S (eds) *New South African Keywords.* Athens (USA): Ohio UP and Auckland Park (SA): Jacana

Wangenge-Ouma G (2008) Globalisation and higher education funding policy shifts in Kenya. *Journal of Higher Education Policy and Management* 30(3): 215–229

Wangenge-Ouma G & Langa PV (2009) Universities and the Mobilization of Claims of Excellence for Competitive Advantage. *Higher Education* 59(6): 749–764

Webometrics (2010) Ranking web of world universities: Top of Africa. Available at: http://www.webometrics.info/top100_continent.asp?cont=africa [accessed 22 November 2010]

Weinrib J (2008) Kant on Citizenship and Universal Independence. *Australian Journal of Legal Philosophy* 33(1): 1–25

WPHE – see Department of Education

Zuern E (2009) Democratization as liberation: Competing African perspectives on democracy. *Democratization* 16(3): 585–603

Appendices

Appendix 1 (Questionnaire UON); Appendix 2 (Questionnaire UCT); Appendix 3 (Questionnaire UCT); Appendix 4 (Conceptual map); Appendix 5 (Statistical sampling factors); Appendix 6 (Regression models and index calculations).

All appendices are available upon request from CHET.